Endorsement

Life in the Heart of God is an invaluable resource for anyone seeking a deeper understanding of God's Word and God's perfect love. Pastor Margaret Duttera is a gifted and insightful teacher who makes the Word of God approachable for the masses. This book is perfect for anyone who has a difficult time interpreting the Bible on their own. In seven chapters Pastor Margaret clarifies what we need to know about God's unconditional love that can help us better comprehend our relationship with our divine creator and each other.

Shelley Sutch
Business Owner and past President of Christ Lutheran Church, San Clemente, California

LIFE
IN THE
HEART
OF GOD

LIFE
IN THE
HEART
OF GOD

A JOURNEY INTO RELEVANT FAITH

Pastor Margaret Duttera

BALBOA.
PRESS

A DIVISION OF HAY HOUSE

ISBN: 978-1-4525-5851-6 (sc)
ISBN: 978-1-4525-5852-3 (e)
ISBN: 978-1-4525-5853-0 (hc)

Library of Congress Control Number: 2012916837

Balboa Press books may be ordered through booksellers or by contacting:

Balboa Press
A Division of Hay House
1663 Liberty Drive
Bloomington, IN 47403
www.balboapress.com
1-(877) 407-4847

Because of the dynamic nature of the Internet, any web addresses or links contained in this book may have changed since publication and may no longer be valid. The views expressed in this work are solely those of the author and do not necessarily reflect the views of the publisher, and the publisher hereby disclaims any responsibility for them.

The author of this book does not dispense medical advice or prescribe the use of any technique as a form of treatment for physical, emotional, or medical problems without the advice of a physician, either directly or indirectly. The intent of the author is only to offer information of a general nature to help you in your quest for emotional and spiritual well-being. In the event you use any of the information in this book for yourself, which is your constitutional right, the author and the publisher assume no responsibility for your actions.

Any people depicted in stock imagery provided by Thinkstock are models, and such images are being used for illustrative purposes only.
Certain stock imagery © Thinkstock.

Printed in the United States of America

Balboa Press rev. date: 11/05/2012

For my family:

my compassionate mother, Mary;

my one-of-a-kind father, Lloyd;

unquestioning support from my entire family;

and for twenty-five years of inspiration and support

from my life partner, Gerri Gordon.

Contents

FOREWORD

From the moment I sat on the rocks with my 3-year old daughter Eve and watched the service unfold, I knew Beach Church was different. The magic created that Sunday morning by the shimmering Pacific, the voices singing joyfully, and the inspiring message from the pastor brought me closer to God than all the years I spent in the Southern Baptist church of my youth. After the service concluded, Eve and I walked down to the water's edge, compelled to meet the people who dared to bring God to the sand. We were immediately welcomed and surrounded by a loving church family.

The true magic of Beach Church was the message that God is for everyone, wherever you are in life.

Life in the Heart of God is the natural extension of the Beach Church experience. Pastor Margaret Duttera shares her experience as a minister, a friend and a witness to God's loving presence in each of us. Her story is easy to understand, and practical in its application in your life. Just as Beach Church drew me in on that gorgeous Sunday morning so long ago, **Life in the Heart of God** will surely draw you in, closer to the God of Love present in us all.

Ginger Silverman

Principal for, Aha! Unlimited Consulting, Inc.
Author, singer, mom, friend.

PREFACE

As far back as I can remember I have been what I think you might call spiritually aware. Was it a result of starting Sunday school at three, or was it an innate awareness? My heart knows it was the latter.

For much of my childhood, I kept my faith to myself, as I realized that my love of Sunday school and church were not shared by most of my childhood friends or my big brother. As the years passed, I always knew that God's love was unconditional, and that God was not far away, but with me always. That knowing made the successes and victories of my life exceptionally joyful, and when my life experiences were hurtful, painful, or frightening, God's loving presence gave me comfort and a sense of ultimate safety.

Reflective and introspective, as I have always been, I spent a lot of quiet time pondering what I would do with my life. Well actually, what I thought God wanted me to do with my life. As you might guess, I wanted to work for God. Well, in the late 1960's, the options for women were limited, to say the least.

After I saw "The Sound of Music", I wanted to become a nun, but I couldn't because I was a renegade Lutheran, not a Roman Catholic. There was one avenue for me to consider. I could become a Lutheran deaconess. Never heard of one? I will spare the details, but if accepted, I would make a vow not to marry, to complete my college degree in education, complete an additional two years of study at Gettysburg Seminary, be consecrated into the Diaconate, and teach in Lutheran schools. I made this decision at 16 and saved the big announcement until Christmas Eve, 1965. My mother cried for joy. My German Lutheran father was furious. He had no intention of spending money to send me to college, and then have me work for nothing. In time, dear old dad adjusted.

I graduated from college, completed my teaching credential, accepted a teaching position at Watsonville High School, and proceeded to complete one summer session class at the Deaconess Mother House in Pennsylvania from a Gettysburg Seminary professor.

While there, I read a quote from Martin Luther, which stated that whatever we do in our daily life is our ministry. That was all I needed to hear. I loved teaching, was having the time of my life teaching, coaching, and interacting with students, so I stayed. My greatest joy was discovering that I was able to integrate my faith into my teaching. I did not explicitly discuss my faith, but simply integrated the fundamental teachings, ways of living and relating, into everything I taught. The results of a spiritually grounded teaching method were evolving young women and men who were affirming of one another, humble in victory, gracious in defeat, patient and understanding of others, trusting, trustworthy, forgiving, and kind.

After about five years, I became aware that a significant number of my students would make good progress in their growth while at school, but that positive behaviors and healthy self-esteem were very quickly undermined at home. These were situations where the family dynamics were counter to the positives that were happening for any particular student while at school. I realized that my impact was limited, partly due to the fact that I only had access to the student, not the family.

In 1970 the Lutheran Church in America approved the ordination of women to be pastors. I left Watsonville High at the end of the school year in 1978. Deep within, I have always known that our lives are inseparably linked to God, whether we have a conscious awareness to that fact or not. To become a Lutheran pastor where I could utilize my gifts as a teacher and have access to whole families was an aha! moment for me. I thought I had figured it all out. I now realize I was on the path with a long way to go.

I just celebrated the 30th anniversary of my ordination as a Lutheran pastor. It took ten years before I realized that vast numbers of people both inside and outside the church, have little life-grounding, life-affirming sense of God's presence in their heart or within their daily life. I realized that traditional religion awakens and nurtures the faith of many, but that today, in the 21st century, vast numbers of people are disconnected, detached or estranged from a life-giving relevant connection to God.

I began to wake up to this reality when the church I was serving in the beach community of San Clemente in California, boldly took church to the beach. "Beach Church" represents the primary motivation for Life in the Heart of God. Taking church to the beach forced an otherwise traditional mainline pastor and people to think outside the box, hold onto what was most relevant, and let go of the rest. In doing so, people who just happened upon this gathering on the beach and dared to sit down on the rocks in the back, were drawn by something they heard, and opened their hearts and minds to a spiritual message that made sense. Some of those sitting on the rocks had grown up in a church, some had not. The miracle was how a chance encounter awakened their spiritual core, and led to their reconnecting with their true spiritual identity. In the process their faith became relevant.

Through Life in the Heart of God you will make a journey. During this journey you will discover what you do and do not believe. You will receive tools to help you discern what you know to be true from within your own heart. The process will enable you to remember who you are, whose you are, and what your specific life is intended to be about. Your personal "spiritual dawn" will emerge and you will be invited to live fully awake within and from the very Heart of God—Home.

I want to acknowledge all those who have asked questions throughout the years, and motivated me to address practices and understandings that I simply accepted. You have helped me to grow in faith and to be far more relevant than I would ever have been on my own.

A special thank you to Joanne McGavran, who after years as my Administrative Ministry Assistant at Christ Lutheran Church in San Clemente, can still read my writing, and sometimes even my mind, in order to make what I have written even better, and who has skillfully handled the technical aspects of preparing the manuscript for Life in the Heart of God for publishing.

INTRODUCTION

We are spiritual beings having a human experience, yet we live as earthbound human beings, with spiritual evolution as one choice on an immense smorgasbord of possible pursuits.

Our experiences with religion or spirituality may have brought us closer to the God of our creation and our true identity, left us distanced at best, or totally disconnected from our spiritual core altogether.

It doesn't matter whether we are ensconced in denominational Christianity, non-denominational church, New Age spirituality, are marginally religious, consider ourselves spiritual rather than religious, atheist or agnostic. Each and every one of us loses our way, experiences times when life overwhelms us, times when we feel isolated, disconnected, insignificant, powerless, alone and fearful.

There is a pathway which will lead us back to our true identity if we are willing to make the journey. Sifting through the stuff of our spiritual foundation, we can bridge the spiritual gap where we have remained hostage to our feelings of isolation, disconnectedness, insignificance, powerlessness, loneliness and fear, enter into our spiritual dawn and awaken within the Heart of God—HOME.

CHAPTER 1

Waking Up

I s faith relevant in your daily life? These pages represent a journey that will put you on a path to Relevant Faith and Life In and From the Heart of God.

Before your birth, where were you? After your body dies, where will you be? You know the answer to both of these questions. Deep within you know, but you have forgotten. You are functioning detached, to some degree, from the source of your existence. I recently asked a ten-year old these same two questions. Without hesitation she answered, "With God" to both questions. I asked the same question of a thirty-year old and he answered this way: "Before I was born I didn't exist and after I die I will be nowhere, just dead." My pastoral heart was uplifted by the answer of the ten-year old and my heart sank when I heard the answer of the 30-year old.

There is undeniably a serious disconnect for many between what traditional religion endeavors to teach and what is internalized and becomes spiritually relevant. Going through the motions, enduring the experience of church, is woefully insufficient to awaken us to the truth of our spiritual identity. For many the faith we hold during childhood is simple, carefree and uncomplicated. As we grow in years, our simple knowing is abandoned and replaced by a flood of contradictory information. Some of the information we receive is the truth, some of it is laced with fear passed on mindlessly from generation to generation, well-intentioned, but fraught with misunderstanding and misinterpretation. Additionally, our personal experience often contradicts what we once believed to be true.

When we were young, information shared with us by someone we trusted, we accepted as fact. As a child I believed everything I was taught in Sunday school.

- God created the world in six days and rested on the seventh.

- God created all people, including me.

- God gave us ten commandments – rules to live by.

- Break any of those commands and God would punish you.

- God caused a flood and saved Noah's family only because they did what God told them to do.

- Jonah didn't do what God said and he was swallowed by a whale.

- Lot's wife disobeyed God and she was turned into a pillar of salt.

- Daniel obeyed God so the lions didn't eat him.

- God sent Jesus because so many people didn't keep God's commands.

- Jesus loved everyone, but because he embarrassed the church leaders they talked Pilot, the Roman Governor, into killing him.

- Jesus died for our sins, but he came back to life so that we would be forgiven and go to heaven, not hell.

Jesus loved me and that's all I needed to know. Then I went to college. Yes, it took that long for me to begin to question my childhood faith. I had a fabulous idea for my Humanities project. I compiled what I was sure would be an awe-inspiring slide show, nature at its best. To top it off I put the entire slide show to music. And not just any music but good old church hymns. The theme of my project was, "Irrefutable Proof of the Existence of God." The room was very quiet and then I detected snickers scattered around the room. I was mortified. How could something that meant so much to me be funny to my peers. Nineteen and naïve as I could be, I did my best to cope with the reality that not everyone found my beliefs to be intellectually credible.

As I began my teaching career I quietly maintained my childhood faith with little alteration. I learned not to talk about it. Secretly, I had wanted to be a pastor from the age of eight or nine. Back then Lutherans did not ordain women. In fact, women were not allowed to hold any office in the church, and little girls were not even allowed to light the candles. Needless to say, I gave up any notion of ever being a pastor, but it didn't stop me from pretending when no one was home.

In 1970 the Lutheran Church in America, to which I belonged, made the landmark decision I had longed for since I was a child. They approved the ordination of women to pastoral ministry, and the first woman was ordained that same year. In 1978 I left my teaching position and entered Pacific Lutheran Theological Seminary in Berkeley, California. I was certain there would be unwavering support for my unquestioned faith within the hallowed halls of this credible traditional institution. Ha! Little did I know I was entering religious boot camp. Piece by piece all the elements of my simplistic Sunday school faith were examined, sifted and reassembled.

One question applied to every biblical text, every doctrine, and every religious practice: What does this mean and how will you interpret and teach this to others? Martin Luther started this whole thought process back in the sixteenth century. "What does this mean?" At thirteen in Confirmation class, I didn't have to answer the question myself. I only had to memorize Luther's response to his own question.

During my seminary years my faith was dismantled and rebuilt. I thought I was all set, but in truth, the transformation of my faith was only beginning. Over the next thirty years as a pastor, endeavoring to empower the faith of others, I became a witness to both the inadequacy of institutional religion to instill relevant faith, and a feeling of futility and resignation among many people of all ages about religious faith all together.

Left to my own natural rhythm, I wake up slowly, gain momentum through the day and truly shine in the evening. The same has been true of my spiritual awakening. It has taken me nearly a lifetime to awaken spiritually. And I attribute my awakening in great part to my own family members, members of the church, friends and even acquaintances.

Waking spiritually is the most fulfilling event of any human life. We are spiritual beings, having a human experience. We have forgotten who we truly are, where we came from, and where we will return. Connecting or reconnecting with the truth frees and empowers us to be not all that we can be, but all that we are. If Christian ancestry, family tradition, personal experience or personal choice have been your essential faith foundation, these pages may provide a pathway that will lead you through the briar patch of traditional religion, to what can become faith, relevant in your daily life, and home to the truth about yourself and God. The gap may be bridged between what you were taught that has not connected and establishing a new understanding related to your spiritual identity.

If you have very little or no specific faith foundation, these pages offer information that will establish a foundation from which your spiritual core will become visible and enable you to connect with your truest identity. You will enter your personal Spiritual Dawn and Life in the Heart of God.

I thought my religious experience had created my faith. I now know that my religious experience supported what was true before my birth and I had forgotten, and to which we all become disconnected to some degree. I invite you to journey with me, creating a bridge from our earthbound reality back to divine truth which transcends space and time.

Story: The Bible

I loved Sunday school. Well, I loved everything except when I was asked to read. Reading was agony for me. I suffered through the humiliation of reading aloud because I loved everything else. I will be forever grateful to a caring teacher who gave me the tools I desperately needed to overcome my difficulty with reading. I loved the songs we sang and putting pennies in the church-shaped bank on my birthday. Everyone would count the pennies as they dropped with a kerplunk into the little white church. I loved praying the Lord's Prayer together and hearing a story from the Bible.

The start of the fourth grade ushered in a series of events that I remember vividly to this very day. That September Rally Day, the first Sunday back after school began in the fall, marked two milestone events.

A. I was now permitted to sit with the fifth and sixth graders in the back two rows.

B. Best of all, this was the day I would receive my very own leather-bound Bible with my name inscribed by none other than our Sunday school superintendent, Miss Catherine Lucas.

To date it was the biggest day of my life. Yes, I have always been a little over the top related to matters of faith. It meant so much to me because I could now read the Bible for myself. And I could read it without embarrassment, struggling to read as I did. I couldn't wait to find that place where it said Jesus loved me. For this little nine-year old raised in the church, I was sure that the whole book was all about love. Turns out it is, when you see it from the Heart of God.

Spiritual Pause (minimum of 5 minutes)

- Find a comfortable place to sit outside or where you can see outside.

- Place a small mirror in your lap, face down.

- Take two or three deep breaths.

- Look, really look at what is around you.

- Everything you see has, in its essence, been created by God. Take it in.

- One creation is of greater value to God than all others.

- Pick up the mirror in your lap, turn it over, hold it at arm's length in your hands.

- You are God's most valued creation.

- You are God's beloved child. Forever.

- Take it in, it is a FACT!

Remember This

You are a spiritual being having a human experience. You have come from God and you will return to God's loving presence. Living from your spiritual essence (love), your life has no limits and you become a healing light in this world.

CHAPTER 2

The Bible: What It Is and What It Is Not

Whether you define yourself as deeply grounded in traditional faith, as marginally religious, spiritual rather than religious, or if you find the whole spectrum of religion irrelevant, taking time to consider what the Bible is as a whole may awaken within you a divine connection that will establish for you a new and profoundly relevant understanding of who you truly are. If you have read the Bible from cover to cover, read only parts of it or none of it, the Bible has influenced your view of life and your part within it.

In western culture the Christian Bible has an explicit impact on those who define themselves as Christian and an implicit impact on those who do not. Basic biblical tenets permeate the fundamental value system of most, whether by conscious choice or simple generic exposure to beliefs such as our having been created by a supernatural force, that actions which harm others are unacceptable, that consequences exist for destructive behavior, and that there is something beyond physical death. One need not be a professed Christian to hold these basic beliefs. What we believe the origin and purpose of the Bible to be and how we interpret what it says accounts for the vast diversity of beliefs and practices within Christianity.

Why are there a multitude of Christian denominations, non-denominational believers, and an infinite number of other "followers of Jesus"? To answer that, let's take a look at what the Bible is and how what it says may be interpreted.

Clarifying Facts

A. What the Bible is

- A collection of 66 individual books.

- 39 Old Testament books, all written before the birth of Jesus.

- 27 New Testament books, all written after the death and resurrection of Jesus.

- The Old Testament books were originally written in Hebrew.

- The New Testament books were originally written in Greek.

- The Bible includes a variety of literary styles: prose, poetry, allegory, parables, laments, song, metaphor, narrative, etc.

- Oral tradition (the verbal sharing passed from generation to generation) preceded written texts by hundreds of generations.

- Some authors are known. Many are not known.

- The first book of the Bible, Genesis, was written between 2000-1500 B.C.

- The Bible is published in many different versions:

  - Translations from the original languages
  - Interpretations of translations
  - Paraphrased versions
  - Summary versions
  - Thematic versions
  - Contemporary language versions of translations, etc.

Examples of four different versions of the Bible

Scripture reading: Matthew 5:14-15

1. Translation from original language, King James Version, Oxford University Press: "Ye are the light of the world. A city that is set on a hill cannot be hidden. Neither do men light a candle and put it under a bushel, but on a candlestick; and it gives light unto all that are in the house."

2. Translation from original language, Revised Standard Version, Oxford University Press: "You are the light of the world. A city set on a hill cannot be hidden. Nor do men light a lamp and put it under a bushel, but on a stand, and it gives light to all in the house."

3. Contemporary language version, translation from original language (based on message expressed rather than the translation of individual words). Living Translation, Touch Point Bible, Guideposts: "You are the light of the world, like a city on a mountain, glowing in the night for

all to see. Don't hide your light under a basket! Instead, put it on the stand and let it shine for all."

4. Contemporary language version, The Message, by Eugene H. Peterson, NAVPRESS: "Here's another way to put it; you're here to be light, bringing out the God colors in the world. God is not a secret to be kept. We're going public with this, as public as a city on a hill. If I make you light bearers, you don't think I'm going to hide you under a bucket, do you? I'm putting you on a light stand."

- More than 1,000 years separates the writing of the earliest book to the last book of the Old Testament.

- The Old Testament relates to the old covenant between God and humanity.

- The New Testament is all about the new covenant between God and humanity through Jesus Christ.

- The entire New Testament was written over a period of about 100 years.

- The first book of the New Testament, the Gospel of Mark, was written about 70 A.D.

B. What the Bible is Not:

- One book.

- Facts, cover to cover.

- Inclusive of the entirety of God's "Word", God's truth revealed to humanity.

- The final "Word" of God.

C. Biblical Content:

- Old Testament:

  - Law: Genesis, Exodus, Leviticus, Numbers and Deuteronomy.
  - Writings: Ruth, Lamentations, Daniel and others.
  - Prophets: Former prophets and latter prophets.

- New Testament:

  - 4 Gospel accounts of the life, death and resurrection of Jesus.
  - Acts of the apostles.
  - 21 books which are letters from various writers after the death and resurrection of Jesus.
  - Revelation, a disclosure, a revealing of God's will for the future.

D. Interpretation, the Great Divide:

- Not all Christians interpret the content of the Bible in the same way.

- How you interpret the Bible dramatically alters your understanding of God's divine intent for all humanity.

Why are there so many different varieties of Christians, different denominations, different church bodies, different understandings of what a Christian church is supposed to be and do?

- All Christians claim the Bible as their Holy Book.

- All Christians say they follow Christ.

- All Christians celebrate Christmas and Easter.

- All Christians say that God created the heaven, the earth and all living things.

- All Christians say that Jesus is the Savior.

On those five things all Christians agree. And that is unfortunately about the totality of what Christians agree on. Who or what is responsible for the differences among Christians? The way individuals and groups interpret the Bible is a central element contributing to diversity.

Below I offer a broad description of two different and distinct ways of interpreting the Bible and how faith is shaped by those interpretations. For some the Bible is inerrant, literally true and directly from God. Those who interpret the Bible in this way represent the most biblically and theologically conservative part of the Christian family. At the other end of the spectrum are those who view the Bible as the inspired Word of God, the living Word. Those who interpret the Bible in this way represent the most biblically and theologically liberal part of the Christian family.

A. The Conservative Approach: Biblical literalism or biblical fundamentalism is the interpretation or translation of the explicit and primary sense of words in the Bible. This method of interpretation often coincides with the belief that the Bible is God's inerrant Word. An example of biblical literal interpretation and inerrancy is that creation occurred in six days exactly as stated.

B. The Progressive Approach: Biblical interpretation based in the historical critical method takes into account when the passage was written, where it was written, its sources, events, places, customs, who is being addressed, and context. The underlying understanding is that reality is universal, accessible to human reason, and that all events historical and natural are interconnected. An example of liberal interpretation would be to embrace the Genesis account of creation as God's revealing divine truth, that God is the creator of all that exists. The focus of understanding is grounded upon how we understand God (our theology) and what the words communicate. The liberal interpreter need not argue six twenty-four hour days. The story supports the belief that God is the Creator.

As we question why there is so much diversity among Christians, additional contributing factors should be considered.

A. Cultural Origins: It makes a difference whether the Christian community/church had its roots in the Middle East, various parts of Europe, Scandinavia, or the United States, and also during which century it evolved.

B. Creeds / Doctrines: Those churches with roots in the early church have as their foundation of belief, and thus practice, many creeds (ancient statements of belief) and doctrines.

- The Roman Catholic Church: Catholicism has doctrines for the Holy Trinity, apostolicity, sacraments, judgment after death, and the Virgin Mary.

- Mainline Protestants: Protestantism is a major grouping within Western Christianity that is not adherent to the same doctrines as the Roman Catholic or Eastern Church. It emerged in sixteenth century Germany from a reaction against medieval Roman Catholic doctrines and practices. Doctrines of the various Protestant denominations vary, but most include "justification by grace through faith alone", "the priesthood of all believers", and "the Bible as the sole authority in all matters of faith and life."

How any given church interprets and understands the Bible sets the foundation for the establishment of everything else a church does in its self-definition, worship and teaching. From my own tradition as a Lutheran pastor, we believe, as stated in the Evangelical Lutheran Church in America constitution, that "This church accepts the canonical scriptures of the Old and New Testaments as the inspired Word of God and the authoritative source and norm of its proclamation, faith and life." The Bible creates and nurtures faith through the work of the Holy Spirit and points us to Jesus Christ as the Living Word of God and Center of our faith. In reading the Bible, we are invited into a relationship with God that both challenges us and promises us new life.

Biblical interpretation, creeds, doctrines, cultural origin, presence or absence of sacraments and tradition, all contribute to the diversity among Christians. Differences are most apparent in worship. In mainline liturgical churches you would experience similarities in terms of service elements. Liturgical churches use a set form or pattern for worship. Liturgy by definition is "the work of the people". Let's take a light-hearted look at liturgical worship through the eyes of "Church-hopping Jake", whose only church experience has been channel surfing on TV. His church hopping is a result of the need to complete a sociology project. This is how Jake summarized his experience.

- **First Stop: Roman Catholic Church:** The head guy is in a dress with a long colored scarf over his shoulders. There are lots of candles, a giant cross with Jesus hanging on it with drops of blood on his head and side. The guy with the scarf must be the priest; he's doing almost all of the talking. We're standing, no we're sitting, no we're kneeling. There's reading from the Bible and now the priest is mixing a drink in a gold cup and holding the biggest, flattest piece of bread I have ever seen. He just said we could come up and get some if we are Catholic. Oh, well. Oh, we are kneeling again. I like what the priest said, but I'm confused.

- **Second Stop: Lutheran Church on the Beach:** I call ahead and ask why they have two worship services. They tell me the one in the church is more formal. I say I went to a Catholic church and they tell me the service in the church is similar to the service at the Catholic church, but that the service on the beach is less formal. I head for the beach. Coffee and donuts are here for the taking—we're off to a good start. Beach chairs, a plain brass cross (no Jesus), music playing. Wow, the guy in charge is a woman. No robe. Well, it is the beach. We're singing, all of us. I don't know the song, but it's a catchy tune. The kids are coming up to sit on a blanket. The woman, she's the pastor, has a puppet. He's funny, the kids love it. I even understand what she said. Oh, we're praying now. The prayer's over, and now the pastor's reading the Gospel, whatever that is. Now she's talking to everyone about the Gospel and what it means. Prayer again. Uh oh, looks like wine and more skinny bread. She says it's for me. I'm invited to come up and have some with everyone else. Everyone is pointing toward the ocean. Wow, a dolphin! Another prayer and she sends us off to love one another. Ya, right!

- **Third Stop: Non-Denominational Mega Church:** This parking lot is huge. A teenager in a florescent vest is pointing me to a parking place and the closest tram stop. "Take the red one for the main service, the blue one for the Rock service, and the orange one for the Youth service." I opt for the red to check out the main service. Wow, hundreds of chairs, a stage and a happening band. Music's playing and the leader's jumping up on the stage in a Hawaiian shirt, khaki pants and deck shoes. "Hi, everyone, I'm Pastor Kyle. Welcome!" There are three giant screens with words to the music and close-ups of the pastor and the band. The pastor's praying like he and God are having a conversation and God is in the balcony. We haven't had to stand up, sit down, or kneel even once. The pastor's announcing that he'll be talking about "Jesus at the wheel". Every now and then he blurts out a question and a few people answer back. We didn't have any wine and flat bread, but I hear there are refreshments in the food court. This whole experience has been a bit confusing, but the one thing I got out of it is that the Bible is an important book if so many people go to so much trouble to talk about it. I think I'll go buy one and read it for myself.

Thanks, Jake, for your insights into diverse worship styles. Let's make the same stops Jake did and see what more we can see.

- **First Stop: Roman Catholic Church:** Priest – male, wearing a white robe with a stole over his shoulders. The color of the stole corresponds to the season of the Christian year. All "liturgical" churches follow the Christian calendar. A priest reads or chants the elements of the service, reads the Gospel, preaches a sermon, presides over the Eucharist. You will stand, sit or kneel as directed. You may sing a hymn, will offer spoken responses in unison and receive the Eucharist (Holy Communion) if you are Roman Catholic.

- **Second Stop: Lutheran Church (ELCA):** The pastor will be a man or woman. In most cases they will also wear a white robe, with a stole appropriate to the season. The service may be formal liturgy or a more contemporary, less formal format. The service will include prayer, scripture reading, sermon by the pastor, Holy Communion for all, and lots of music. Be prepared to sing. And, oh yes, there will be an offering. If the service is all inclusive, you will be invited to participate in a confession of sins and receive an absolution. There will most likely be a special message for the children. It may be your favorite part. Check the list of events, there will be food somewhere.

- **Third Stop: Non-Denominational Mega Church:** Arrive early, there may be thousands in attendance. There will likely be volunteers to help you find a parking place. The worship space may or may not look like a traditional church sanctuary. You will sit in chairs, not pews. The pastor, most likely a man, will be dressed informally. There will be music, a band or guitars, and large projection screens on the walls. There will be prayer, reading from the Bible, a message and prayer to send you out into the world. There will likely be several options in terms of worship style; participation in Bible studies will be encouraged.

Story: Real Life

The service on the beach had just ended. I was gathering my folder, Rufus, my alter-ego puppet, assorted props, and putting my lapel mic away in its carrying case, ready to head for the 10:30 service at the church when Ryan approached. He had tears in his eyes and looked a little hesitant as he approached. "Could we get together and talk?" he asked. "Of course," I responded.

We met on the beach later that week. Still hesitant, Ryan swallowed hard and shared that he hadn't had much experience with church stuff. He said he really liked the sermons, but the rest of the stuff he wasn't so sure about. Did he have to believe it all to be a member of the church? Ryan, like so many, longed to believe that the unconditional love he was hearing about was available to him, too.

God attempted to keep things simple for us so that we would remember who we are, who God is, and what this earthly life is about. But we, the created ones, have vociferated to the point of making it difficult to get to the core truths God longs to communicate to us.

What kinds of questions did Ryan ask:

A. Must I believe that creation happened in six days?

B. Virgin birth? I don't get it.

C. Why in that creed did we say that Jesus went to Hell first?

D. Is Heaven a real place?

E. Can I go to Heaven only if I'm perfect?

F. Do I have to believe everything in the Bible literally?

G. Why do I have to confess my sins every week?

H. Is it okay if I only come to church on the beach? I'm uncomfortable in the church building. I don't know what all that stuff means.

Interpreting the Bible as the inspired Word of God which creates and nurtures faith and is illumined through Jesus Christ, who creates a pathway for us to return home to God and God's divine intent for our life journey, is no easy task. God's Word is not static, but living. Ryan's question might well be addressed in this way:

1. The six-day creation account, at its root, establishes the core belief that God is the creator of all life.

2. The proclamation of the virgin birth of Jesus affirms God's omnipotence, acknowledging that God is all powerful and can do what, for humans, is impossible. God is the sole creator and is all-powerful.

3. Those known as the early church fathers who created the creeds (statements of what a follower of Jesus believes) endeavored to establish the fact that Jesus was fully human and fully divine, God incarnate (God with us). In the Apostles' Creed (statement of what a Christian believes about God, Jesus and the Holy Spirit), the writers' statement that Jesus "was crucified, died and was buried, and descended into hell…" establishes Jesus' humanity. "On the third day he rose from the dead and ascended into heaven," establishes Jesus' divinity.

4. The answer based on biblical descriptions, biblical teaching, is yes. Whether it is earth-like, minus pain and suffering, may miss the intent of Jesus' life, death and resurrection. To be in heaven is to return to the place from which we came, the very heart of God.

5. If so, we are in trouble. The purpose of Jesus' life was to guide us back to God's intent for our earthly life, and ultimately home to the heart of God. Jesus assures us that we are forgiven when we repent (turn away from what separates us from God's intent), and forgiven we are given the gift of new life again and again.

6. The Bible is the inspired Word of God, illumined through Jesus, God's Living Word. Interpreting every word literally does not allow God to speak in the present. The time period when a biblical passage was written, who was writing, what issues were being experienced, cultural customs, and context all matter. Jesus Christ is the lens through which all biblical material must be focused.

7. Confessing sin (anything which separates us from God's loving intent) helps us acknowledge to ourselves where we are in need of adjusting, redirecting our thoughts, words and actions. It also keeps us grounded in the reality that we are the created, dependent upon God's benevolent spirit providing everything we need to sustain our life and to bring us joy and fulfillment. Through confession and forgiveness we are refocused in our individual lives to fulfill our divine purpose.

8. God never intended for us to create religious "institutions". Jesus endeavored to teach us that we "are the church", individually and together. To "be the church" is "to be the body of Christ." We are the body of Christ when we follow Jesus' teaching and example in our individual lives. Going to a particular church ought to be about participating in a faith community

where we encounter God, where our faith is nurtured, where who we are, whose we are, and what our life is intended to be are clarified and affirmed. If church on the beach is that place—Alleluia!

It's easy to be a pastor to people who were raised in the church and readily buy the whole enchilada. It is quite another thing to interpret the heart of divine truth when we have created a colossal obstacle course with ancient scriptures, creeds, doctrines, liturgical practices, sacraments, religious rites, centuries of old hymns, theology and confessions. For many today, traditional religion is unnecessary at best, if not altogether irrelevant.

When faith makes sense, when faith is relevant in our daily life, who we are, whose we are, and the purpose of our life become clear. It is then that our journey is most fulfilling, grounded and motivated by love, filled with joy, gratitude and inner peace.

Spiritual Pause (minimum of 10 minutes)

- Look or step outside, find a comfortable place to sit and take a deep breath.

- Focus on everything living.

- Breathe.

- Genesis 1:1 "In the beginning God created the heavens and the earth."

- Breathe.

- God created you.

- Breathe.

- There is no one of greater value to God than you.

- Breathe.

- God, the creator of all life, loves you.

- Breathe.

- God is love. You are love.

- Breathe.

- Love is all that God is.

- Love is all that you are.

- Breathe. Take it in.

- As you breathe in, God's infinite, unconditional love fills you.

- Take it in.

Remember This

The Bible is a gift. Within the Bible is a record of God's presence throughout time. Reading and studying through the words and teachings of Jesus, you understand that God is loving and gracious. Most importantly, you are reminded of God's love for all people. The Bible awakens you to the truth of who you are, whose you are, and what you are to be about on this earth.

CHAPTER 3

The Bible of Jesus

Jesus didn't have a Bible. What Jesus had were essentially the scriptures of the Old Testament, known as the Pentateuch, the first five books of the Old Testament, the books of the Law.

I'd love to sit down with Jesus and ask him what he thinks about the entire collection of scriptures that were selected to be included in the "Bible". I venture that Jesus would be both pleased and mildly perplexed. Jesus spent a significant amount of time speaking to and endeavoring to illumine the actual meaning of the Old Testament texts. While the texts established a foundation of understanding about God and God's will, they were sometimes misinterpreted, and consequently distorted God's true intent. When questioned about certain passages, specific laws of faith, Jesus would respond, frequently offering interpretations which did not square with the understanding of the texts or laws by the religious leaders of the day. Those conflicts of interpretation ultimately led to Jesus being labeled a heretic, an uncontrollable radical, and prompted the zealous Jewish religious leaders to incite the people to demand that the Roman governor have Jesus crucified.

The Bible of Jesus, the Old Testament, is perhaps better understood when we use the original word "covenant", which for us equates with "promise". Jesus, born of Jewish parents, was raised within the Jewish community of Nazareth in Galilee. There was no Old Testament Bible, but collections of scrolls protected and preserved within the temple. Jesus was educated at the synagogue where the scrolls were read. The scriptures to which Jesus was exposed, and which ultimately make up the Old Testament today, represent a literary expression of the religious life of ancient Israel. The scriptures cover the time from creation through the Israelite sojourn and captivity in Egypt, the exodus, divine law, the writings of the prophets and other writings.

The Old Testament-Covenant is all about the relationship God establishes with his people. The specific scriptures which were the foundation of Jesus' education include the story of creation, the fall into sin, Noah and the great flood, God's call to Abraham, God's promise to Abraham, Israel's bondage in Egypt, Moses, the first Passover, the exodus from Egypt, the wilderness journey in search of the Promised Land, Moses receiving the Ten Commandments, the covenant code, the laws. In total, the Old Testament as we have it today was the five books of the Law, the prophets, and writings. Most notable among the writings are the books of Ruth, Job, Daniel, and Jonah.

Interpreting and understanding Old Testament theology (our understanding of God) and integrating them into our 21st century lives is not an easy endeavor. Simply claiming it is all literally factual and that it all applies today, exactly as it did as many as 3,500 or so years ago, limits God's activity to ancient history and defeats God's intent to have a relationship with us at this moment in time.

During the time period that the Bible was written, the world was understood in vastly different ways. Of profound importance is the understanding of nature. What we consider natural occurrences today were, in biblical times, attributed to God: rain, hail, flood, drought, earthquake, lightening, thunder, disease, physical deformity, blindness, barrenness, etc. God was seen as an angry God, vengeful and retaliatory, using everything at his disposal to punish.

When Jesus enters into human history Jesus reveals God's true nature and turns centuries of belief related to God's divine intent upside down. One of the most poignant biblical passages that Jesus redefines is in the Old Testament book of Deuteronomy 19:21: "Your eye shall not pity; it shall be life for life, eye for eye, tooth for tooth, hand for hand, foot for foot." In Matthew 5:38 in the New Testament, Jesus illumines the loving nature of God with these words: "You have heard that it was said, 'An eye for an eye and a tooth for a tooth.' But I say to you, do not resist one who is evil. But if anyone strikes you on the right cheek, turn to him the other also; and if anyone would sue you and take your coat, let him have your cloak as well; and if anyone forces you to go one mile, go with him two miles. Give to him who begs from you, and do not refuse him who would borrow from you". Jesus *knew* the scriptures. Jesus *knew* the Laws of scripture. Most importantly, Jesus *knew* the Heart of God. That knowing changed everything!

Story: Kids' Thoughts on the Bible

Twelve-year old girl: "Pastor, let me get this straight. God made Adam and Eve, and Cain and Abel were their sons, right? So, who made God?"

Fourteen-year old girl: "We are studying evolution in my science class. Scientific evidence says it took millions of years to create the earth, so what's with the six-day version in the Bible? What am I supposed to believe?"

Ten-year old boy confiding in a friend: "Did you hear those 10 commandments? I'm doomed. I said a bad word when I forgot my homework at home. I went to a soccer game instead of church last week. I told my dad he was like a prison guard. I put a match down an ant hole, stole my sister's cookies out of her lunch, blamed the uncle who visited from Texas for leaving the light on in the basement, and told the owner of the sporting goods store I couldn't buy the glove I needed to be able to play baseball because my parents had been killed by an avalanche while on a trip to Alaska, so he gave me a glove. The only commandment I haven't broken is the one about adultery. I don't know what that is, but I'm sure to do it someday. I just know I'll never see heaven."

Context matters. Interpretation is of critical importance.

Spiritual Pause (minimum of 10 minutes)

- Place your book on your lap and your hands open, palms up.

- Relax and breathe.

- You were created in the image of God. Gaze at your hands.

- Before your birth you were with God. Gaze at your hands.

- God is present with you every moment. Gaze at your hands.

- When you die you will be with God. Gaze at your hands.

- Your hands are God's hands. You have been blessed to be a blessing in the life of everyone who comes into your life.

- God's love flows through your hands.

- Feel the love radiate in your hands now.

- Be the love God created you to be.

Remember This

The holy writings available to Jesus primarily included what we know as the first five books of the Old Testament of the Bible, writings of the prophets and stories. Jesus in his teaching clarified and expanded upon God's will and divine intent. The sacred writings were the foundation of Jesus' teaching and represented the history of Israel. The Messiah, the Savior, was expected to redeem Israel. Jesus fulfills God's divine intent, not only for Israel, but for the whole human family.

CHAPTER 4

Jesus Changes Everything

For the remainder of this book, suspend your current opinions about the Bible and open your mind and heart to experience the Bible through the Heart of Jesus. The Bible experienced through the Heart of Jesus is an unobstructed window through which we see clearly the very Heart of God. Rather than a vault holding unequivocal, once-and-for-all finite divine decrees, the Bible, embraced as an unobstructed window, allows the light of Jesus to reveal God's true identity and divine will for all humanity. The Bible, if embraced and internalized in this way, awakens us beyond the limited capacity of our individual minds, to see the infinite through the eyes of Jesus, and discover the very Heart of God.

With suspended biblical opinion, allow this simple summary of ideas and images to pass before the unobstructed window of your heart:

- God created the heavens and the earth.

- God created you (in love).

- God is love.

- Love is the only thing that God is.

- Created by God, in God's image and likeness, love is all that you are.

Once born, for a brief time, when you were very young, you knew innately who you were: the "center of the universe", with a twist. Human, in physical form, you were dependent. To have your physical life sustained, you needed to rely on other physical beings outside of your essential self. That physical dependence placed you in a very vulnerable position where you had little control. During the early years of your life, you automatically processed every experience. Based on your experience you made judgments about yourself and others.

In Western culture, by our teens and early twenties we tend to believe we have it all figured out. Often our early sense of self is lost. Our knowing becomes clouded by messages which create doubt and fear. We abandon unconsciously what we once knew, and embark on a journey which does not always lead us back to the *truth*. The *truth* never changed.

- God created the heavens and the earth.

- God created you (in love).

- God is love.

- Love is the only thing God is.

- Created by God, in God's image and likeness, love is all that you are.

You have forgotten who you are. The thoughts of your mind have betrayed you. I have learned that it wasn't my distant, never-impressed father, it wasn't my indecisive passive mother who were the cause of my "forgetting". It wasn't the humiliation of being in the lowest reading group. It wasn't abuse I endured or the lingering fear that I just wasn't very smart. It wasn't anything that happened to me, but the thoughts of my mind about those things and the choices I made as a result of my thoughts. The same is true for you! Out of this kind of clouded reality we continue to live out our lives, unless we awaken and remember the truth.

You are a spiritual being on an earthly journey. Religion/ spiritual pursuits do not give you the truth, but they can help you remember what you have forgotten about who you truly are. Jesus changes everything by sifting out the unnecessary and inaccurate notions about who God is, who we are, and what this earthly journey is about, for every child of God.

Jesus himself is the lens through which every experience, every encounter, every word of scripture can be seen and understood with clarity.

With the birth of Jesus, God does something totally new. No longer will God raise up prophets in an effort to wake us up to our true identity. Now God intervenes in human history as never before. God incarnate (present) in Jesus, comes and lives among us. Immanuel, God with us! God is inexplicably revealed to us in the words and actions of Jesus. The Bible is now more than a collection of texts, it's "the cradle of Christ", as stated by Martin Luther. Now, every word is illumined by Jesus.

Jesus changes everything forever in the final day of his earthly life. Jesus gets together with his closest friends and they share a meal. After they eat, Jesus picks up a loaf of bread in his hands, looks at his friends and tells them that the bread represents his body, and that he is going to give up his body for them; that when they are together after he is gone, he wants them to share this bread with one another. Then Jesus takes a cup of wine in his hands and as he shares it with them, he tells them that the wine represents a new promise; that his blood, which he would shed for them, is for the forgiveness of sin, all those things which create separation between us and the God of our creation. Jesus returns us to divine truth. Nothing separates us from the love of God. It is Jesus who enables us to reclaim our true identity.

Lutheran theology states that we are saved by grace through faith alone. If we understand faith at its very core to be *knowing*, not simply hoping, but the acknowledgement, the claiming of divine truth, then Yes!

Jesus changes everything because he shows us by his death and resurrection and return to physical form the infinite, eternal reality of the power of love. When Jesus says, "I am the way, the truth and the life", he is not saying follow me and I will tell you the truth and you will have eternal life. Jesus is telling us that the way, truth and life are a continuum, a never ending circle of truth. When he adds, "No one comes to the father but by me", it is not a threat to avoid hell, but another glimpse into God's identity reminding us who we all are: children of the One God.

Jesus changes everything forever, but generally speaking, we still don't get it. Jesus has illumined our common humanity and divine origin, yet we have claimed the right understanding of Jesus as yet another requirement in order to benefit from what Jesus simply gives away: the truth about who we are. Jesus changes everything, assuming we claim as our own the insight and gift he offers.

Story: Ade

He had been a faithful church-going man his whole life. He was the kind of person everyone wanted to be around. He always smiled, he was always happy to see you, always interested in what was going on in your life. When Ade came into the room, his positive energy was like an infusion of fresh air. Ade never missed an event. He not only attended, he always helped. His beloved wife Margaret died shortly before I became his pastor. Ade had always been healthy and strong. He was in his nineties when his health began to decline. His heart was failing and he was too frail for any intervention, so he was sent home from the hospital under Hospice care. The final time I saw Ade, he was unable to speak, very ill at ease and had a look of anxiety and fear on his face. I couldn't imagine that there was anything in Ade's past that would cause him to be so fearful. I held his hand and reassured him that God knew everything he had ever done, that God loved him unconditionally, and there was nothing to fear. Ade's hand relaxed, his frown disappeared and he took a long deep breath. The next day I called to see how he was doing. His daughter asked apologetically, "Didn't anyone call you? Dad died peacefully about twenty minutes after you left."

Jesus changes everything, if we listen!

Spiritual Pause (minimum of 5 minutes)

Sit in a quiet place with your hands resting in your lap with your palms up.

Now, see yourself standing before the gates of heaven. St. Peter smiles and asks you one simple question: "Is there a reason you have not walked through the gate into heaven?"

You try to remember. You know there are plenty of reasons you should not be welcome here. You are sure you failed to be all that you could be, but no matter how hard you try, you cannot think of a single thing. "I can't seem to remember, St. Peter."

"Sweet child," he responds, "that's because God holds only the love which has always been within you. God is delighted to have you home where love is truly the only reality."

Jesus changes everything!

Remember This

Jesus is the Savior of the world. As you make this earthly journey, Jesus (Immanuel, God with us) provides a path upon which every human being is invited to travel. Jesus Christ cannot be contained within institutional creeds, doctrines, traditions, rites, worship practices, or selective ethnic or cultural origins. Christ is bigger than that. The Christ, the Savior of the world, the way home, exists asleep or awake within you. Christ, God incarnate, the creator of all, exists within Christians and—hold onto your hats—within every human heart.

It is not the "correct" belief that saves you, but faith (knowing) that God's all-powerful love and loving intent for you and all humanity is fully revealed in Jesus Christ.

Jesus changes everything!

CHAPTER 5

God Post-Scripture

Now hear this:

- God did not cease speaking at the end of the Bible.

- God speaks through all of his children who live from love.

- Christ did not vanish. The Holy Spirit, God's empowering presence, is as present today as ever. It is within.

- Divine truth is found in surprising places, within and far beyond the framework of traditional theology and faith.

Consider this: The texts that comprise the Old and New Testament of the Bible were compiled and put into current form as the Bible, nearly 2,000 years ago. Yes, God is inexplicably present and revealed within the Bible, but not only within the pages of the book as we know it. When we hold only to the God of ancient history, we drastically discount the enormity of God's creative reality in the universe. God was present and revealed long before the first word of scripture was written, and God has been present and continues to be revealed moment by moment by moment. Not only is God revealed every moment, God also continues to create and participate in our world and in our individual lives.

God speaks loudly! We listen selectively!

By limiting God's word to ancient scripture, we have essentially put God in solitary confinement. Confined to existing biblical interpretation, the Bible can become a very narrow filter that may keep us marginally on God's path, but may well filter out God's attempts to speak to us in the 21st century and beyond. If we seek God only within the books of the Bible as God's final word, I fear we will awaken spiritually no further. The Bible interpreted literally can become an impenetrable vault, confining God to ancient understanding and denying Christ's teaching of God's true identity, which guides us back to love, back to the Heart of God—Home!

Jesus himself speaks of "the great cloud of witnesses", past, present and future. God is infinite in every regard:

- Infinite in creative power.

- Infinite in compassion and love.

- Infinite in time and space, as we understand them.

Our very existence is a miracle. We are spiritual in essence, yet physical beings. No traditional theology speaks of this reality in a way that most people are able to understand or internalize. Birth and death are physical realities we understand. Where we were before birth, and where we will be after our physical death remain uncertain, except by faith. In the midst of our lives, we forget who we are. The physical world consumes us and fear causes us to accept a god (small "g" intended), who is judgmental, vengeful, punishing, excludes the unrighteous, and is accessible to only a select group who believe rightly. **"And Jesus weeps."**

Scripture is holy in as far as it reflects the God whom Jesus strives endlessly to reveal to us. The good news is that God is love. Love is all that God is. Today God's Living Word is present in ancient texts and through the sons and daughters of light in every corner of the earth. Christ is alive in many places. Awakening to the vast dimensions and presence of God, our faith becomes relevant, an unobstructed pathway to life in and from the Heart of God and our own personal Spiritual Dawn.

Story: Spiritual Evolution

Kevin had never before sat down one on one with his pastor, but he felt he owed him that much before he left the church of his childhood for good. The pastor welcomed him with a broad smile and sincere hug. "Pastor, my faith has changed and I wanted to share with you how." Kevin had entered the pastor's office with several books tucked under his arm. "I want to show you what I have been reading. When we entered the fourth grade, you gave us the King James Version of the Bible. You know, the one with all of the thee and thou pronouns?" The pastor smiled and nodded.

"Well, this is my new Bible." Kevin placed the Message translation of the Bible on the pastor's desk. "Pastor, I love this one." After placing his hand on the Bible Kevin had placed before him, the pastor said, "Just last Sunday I read the passage that I used for my sermon from this very translation." "Really?" Kevin replied in surprise. Next Kevin placed a book by Thich Naht Hanah, Living Buddha, Living Christ on the pastor's desk. The pastor picked it up and smiling said, "Isn't this an amazing intricate weaving of our spiritual connectedness?"

This was not going the way Kevin thought it would go. Kevin was sure this next book would definitely be met with disapproval. Slowly Kevin placed the book entitled A Course in Miracles before the pastor. The pastor held the book in his hands silently for several moments, then looked up at Kevin and said, "Kevin, it's right, you know. 'Love is the only true reality.' Jesus endeavored to teach us that."

Kevin could hardly believe what he was hearing. Was it possible that his new spiritual awareness was not really new, but part of a natural spiritual journey that had evolved from his traditional roots? Kevin swallowed, took a deep breath and forged ahead. There was one last book on Kevin's lap. Silently he placed it before the pastor, The New Earth, by Ekhart Tolle. Again the pastor was smiling. Kevin was so certain that his spiritual journey and present understanding of who God is, what the Bible teaches, Jesus and all the rest of his evolving spiritual journey made him a heretic in relation to traditional religious teaching. Kevin had come to see his pastor one final time, certain that he had grown beyond everything represented by his childhood community of faith.

"Kevin, Kevin!" (Kevin was lost in his thought.) "This book is a powerful affirmation of who we truly are. It helps us understand how and why we get lost during our life and how we can find our way back to who we truly are and move into a new place personally and spiritually.

For several moments Kevin said nothing. Slowly Kevin raised his head, tears running down his cheeks. "Pastor, I thought my spiritual journey had taken me beyond the allowable limits of what I had once believed, and that the only honorable thing for me to do was to leave the church. It never occurred to me that my faith foundation, examined and understood in the light of Christ, was a continuum, a journey really. I am in a totally new spiritual place, but I know that I am home, back in the Heart of God. I need some time to process all of this. Can we talk again?"

Pastor Frank's eyes were filled with love and utter delight. "Kevin, you have grown beyond literal interpretation and are awakening where faith which evolves becomes deep knowing. I'm proud of you Kevin, very proud. Let's talk again soon."

As Kevin rose and turned to leave, Pastor Frank remarked, "Kevin, you are on the path. Continue your spiritual quest. You have entered your Spiritual Dawn."

At the present time Kevin continues to read spiritual books from a diverse array of authors and traditions. Kevin still attends the church of his youth twice a month. On the first and third Sunday of every month Kevin leads a class entitled "Spiritual Dawn". The class description: A Journey Into Relevant Faith. The class participants: a group of thirty, growing in numbers, diverse in age and background.

Spiritual Pause (minimum 20 minutes)

Settle into a comfortable, bright location. Read each of the listed passages with an open heart and mind. Attempt to read each passage as though it is the very first time you have ever heard these life-affirming truths.

Read the passages as listed:

Genesis 1:1-6 (New Revised Standard Version):

In the beginning when God created the heavens and the earth, the earth was a formless void and darkness covered the face of the deep, while a wind from God swept over the face of the waters. Then God said, "Let there be light"; and there was light. And God saw that the light was good; and God separated the light from the darkness. God called the light Day, and the darkness he called Night. And there was evening and there was morning, the first day. And God said, "Let there be a dome in the midst of the waters, and let it separate the waters from the waters."

Reflection:

- God has created everything you see before you. Look around! Breathe deeply.

- God, in perfect balance, sustains all life. Place your finger on your pulse. Close your eyes, feel the beat of your heart. Breathe deeply.

- God creates continuously. Look at the top of your hand. See the pathway moving life through your body. Breathe deeply.

- You are God's creation. Magnificent! Breathe deeply.

Exodus 20:1-17 (The Message):

God spoke all these words: I am God, your God, who brought you out of the land of Egypt, out of a life of slavery. No other gods, only me. No carved gods of any size, shape, or form of anything whatever, whether of things that fly or walk or swim. Don't bow down to them and don't serve them because I am God, your God, and I'm a most jealous God, punishing the children for any sins their parents pass on to them to the third, and yes, even to the fourth generation of those who hate me. But I'm unswervingly loyal to the thousands who love me and keep my commandments. No using the name of God, your God, in curses or silly banter; God won't put up with the irreverant use of his name. Observe the Sabbath day, to keep it holy. Work six days and do everything you need to do. But the seventh day is a Sabbath to God, your God. Don't do any work - not you, nor your son, nor your daughter, nor your servant, nor your maid, nor your animals, not even the foreign guest visiting in your town. For in six days God made Heaven, Earth, and sea, and everything in them; he rested on the seventh day. Therefore God blessed the Sabbath day; he set it apart as a holy day. Honor your father and mother so that you'll live a long time in the land that God, your God, is giving you. No murder. No adultery. No stealing. No lies about your neighbor. No lusting after your neighbor's house - or wife or servant or maid or ox or donkey. Don't set your heart on anything that is your neighbor's.

Reflection:

Repeat each statement three times slowly:

- God intervened in human history so that I might remember who and whose I am, and experience the love and joy that God intends for me and every child of the earth.

- I am God's beloved child.

- The commandments are an awesome gift. They are not threats of retribution, but the key elements of God's divine intent for my life. Faithful to God's loving intent, I am continually empowered with love.

John 14:1-7 (The Message):

Jesus said: "Don't let this throw you. You trust God, don't you? Trust me. There is plenty of room for you in my Father's home. If that weren't so, would I have told you that I'm on my way to get a room ready for you? And if I'm on my way to get your room ready, I'll come back and get you so you can live where I live. And you already know the road I'm taking." Thomas said, "Master, we have no idea where you're going. How do you expect us to know the road?" Jesus said, "I am the Road, also the Truth, also the Life. No one gets to the Father apart from me. If you really knew me, you would know my Father as well. From now on, you do know him. You've even seen him!"

With each breath, internalize the truth revealed by Jesus:

- Jesus is Immanuel (God with us). On this earthly journey I have forgotten my true identity.

- Jesus reveals to me who I am, where I have come from and where I will be always.

- The way, the truth and life that are eternal are revealed in Jesus and are my inheritance.

- Jesus is standing before me. Jesus is smiling and his eyes are filled with unconditional, infinite love!

Matthew 22:34-40 (The Message):

When the Pharisees heard how he had bested the Sadducees, they gathered their forces for an assault. One of their religion scholars spoke for them, posing a question they hoped would show him up: "Teacher, which command in God's Law is the most important?" Jesus said, "Love the Lord your God with all your passion and prayer and intelligence. This is the most important, the first on any list. But there is a second to set alongside it: Love others as well as you love yourself. These two commands are pegs; everything in God's Law and the Prophets hangs from them."

Reflection:

- Imagine looking directly into the face of Jesus.

- What are you to be and do in this life? LOVE!

- What will your love create? Your love will contribute to the expansion of love in the world as God intends.

- Reflect again on these three thoughts.

Psalm 23 (Revised Standard Version):

A Psalm of David. The Lord is my shepherd, I shall not want; he makes me lie down in green pastures. He leads me beside still waters; he restores my soul. He leads me in paths of righteousness for his name's sake. Even though I walk through the valley of the shadow of death, I fear no evil; for thou art with me; thy rod and thy staff, they comfort me. Thou preparest a table before me in the presence of my enemies; thou anointest my head with oil, my cup overflows. Surely goodness and mercy shall follow me all the days of my life; and I shall dwell in the house of the Lord forever.

Reflection:

- God is speaking directly to you now!

- You are never without My love.

- Stay awake to My unconditional loving presence. You are entering into your Spiritual Dawn and returning to My heart.

- I am with you, My love is within you, moment, by moment, by moment.

- Repeat these phrases often. Hear God's voice.

Remember This

God continues to create and participate in your world and in your individual life, day by day, by day. Birth and death are physical realities you understand. Where you were before birth, and where you will be after your physical death remains uncertain, except by faith. In the midst of your life, you forget who you truly are. Awakening to the vast dimensions and presence of God, your faith becomes relevant, an unobstructed pathway to life in and from the Heart of God and your own personal Spiritual Dawn.

- God is the creator of all life.

- God's divine intent is that all humanity live from love, respecting self and others.

- You have come from God and you will return to God. That is a promise.

- You are to love others as God loves you.

- There is nothing to fear. God is with you in love, always and forever.

CHAPTER 6

Your Spiritual Dawn

Waking Up:

Awakening to the reality that faith does not, in fact cannot remain static, has for me been the first step in the ongoing evolution of my personal Spiritual Dawn. That reality, however, was only the first step in an ongoing journey. My process toward awakening spiritually was not so much a choice as an essential requirement if I were to ever shepherd others toward relevant faith, later understood as true knowing.

Remembering who you are, who you truly are, is every bit as important for you as it has been for me. When you allow this physical world, which is finite, to obscure your ability to see the infinite, you fall victim to your fears. When you understand your life on this earth as a progressive journey from divine light to divine light, your Spiritual Dawn emerges, and you experience the innate power of divine love within you.

The Bible:

The Bible is by definition in my Lutheran denomination, "the source and norm of our faith and life". I never questioned any part of the Bible until my seminary professors began to ask tough questions. For all the years since seminary I have endeavored to faithfully discern what the Bible is and what it is not, doing so with Christ as the viewing lens. Deep in my heart I believe that by using both a zoom lens and a wide angle lens in studying the Bible, God's intent for all humanity becomes more clear. It is Jesus whose teaching and example, birth, death and resurrection offer divine clarity. Jesus becomes the reference source for every word of scriptural text.

The Bible of Jesus:

The Old Testament can no longer stand alone once Jesus, God incarnate, breaks into human history and the human heart. The Old Testament establishes the essential foundation for understanding human origin and our relationship to God, the creator of all life. It is from that foundation that Jesus reveals God's true identity and begins the process that brings us back to the truth of our identity.

Jesus Changes Everything:

Existing theology (understanding of God) and the religious establishment are literally turned upside down and inside out by the teaching of Jesus. Where the description of God and God's intent for humanity is accurate, Jesus affirms it. Where the understanding of God and God's intent is inaccurate or misinterpreted, Jesus corrects it. To this very day, self-centered as we are, we typically accept what serves our purposes and ignore or explain away whatever we don't like.

From Exodus 21:23-24 of the Old Testament (RSV): "If any harm follows, then you shall give life for life, eye for eye, tooth for tooth, hand for hand, foot for foot, burn for burn, wound for wound, stripe for stripe."

From Matthew 5:38-42 of the New Testament (RSV), Jesus says, "You have heard that it was said, 'An eye for an eye, and a tooth for a tooth.' But I say to you, do not resist one who is evil. But if anyone strikes you on the right cheek, turn to him the other also; and if anyone would sue you and take your coat, let him have your cloak as well; and if anyone forces you to go one mile, go with him two miles. Give to him who begs from you, and do not refuse him who would borrow from you."

In reality, we find much of what Jesus teaches offensive! In our opinion, some of what Jesus espouses is simply not realistic. "Love your enemies", outrageous! And those two examples represent only two examples in a very long list. If we believe that what Jesus teaches is divine truth and align ourselves with that truth, then and only then, is everything changed by Jesus, because then Jesus changes us.

God Post-Scripture:

The Bible is the Living Word of God! It establishes a foundation of understanding about who we are, who God is and what this life is truly to be about. As Living Word it is not the culmination of God's interaction with humanity, but the beginning. God speaks within the Bible, in creation, in the human heart, and in ways we have yet to comprehend. God is alive and present.

Spiritual Dawn:

Our Spiritual Dawn begins to be visible in the distance when we understand the Book (the Bible), the ancient world, and the transforming reality established by Jesus. As we awaken we remember who we are, where we came from and to where we will return. Fear diminishes, our vision clears, peace descends upon us, gratitude and joy radiate within us and from us.

Entering into your personal Spiritual Dawn is a choice, a decision you must make deep within your heart. Within the Heart of God, there is only love. Rest there. Be still and know, be still and know.

Story: One With the Sea, One With God

Moments when we can be both observer and participant within this awesome creation transform us. Imagine yourself resting comfortably on a beautiful beach. You are gazing between two tall palm trees at the golden sand, at the glistening blue sea, as small waves break just off shore. There is a gentle breeze, the sky is pastel blue and there are white fluffy clouds passing over your head. The sound of the waves breaking, rolling up the beach and gently rolling back into the sea soothes your soul. In these precious moments, in this place you are poised at the threshold of your Spiritual Dawn, which illumines a pathway into the very Heart of God. This convergence of earth, sea and sky captures the living presence of God. The journey from your Spiritual Dawn into the Heart of God is vividly illustrated by the natural rhythm of the sea.

Imagine now a surfer, abandoning the security of solid ground and merging with the sea. Entering the water, the surfer knows to observe the movement of the waves, pushing off into the water as the largest in a set of breakers runs back into the heart of the sea. The sea in retreat assists the surfer out into deeper water, where the surfer paddles to establish a resting place outside the breaking waves. The surfer doesn't challenge the large breaking waves, but ducks into the breaker, allowing it to pass over the top of her or him.

Patiently the surfer waits to join with an incoming wave as it completes its journey to the shore. The surfer joins the energy generated by the wave and experiences being a part of the wave. It is exhilarating to be one with the sea, to be one with God.

Your Spiritual Dawn is not a destination, but a perpetual state of being and becoming. You are supported, carried, progressing forward propelled by a power more vast than the sea. It is not a religion, not a belief, not a doctrine of faith. It is a knowing deeper than any thought. It is your heart within the Heart of God.

Spiritual Pause (minimum of 10 minutes)

Sit in a comfortable chair at a table with a lighted candle in front of you. Take a deep breath. Hear God's loving voice. Continue to focus on the light of the candle.

- Be still and know.

- I have created you in love.

- Be still and know.

- My love is within you.

- Be still and know.

- I am only love.

- Be still and know.

- I am with you, loving you every moment.

- Be still and know.

- Focus upon the light before you.

- Join the light.

- Breathe and remain within the light.

- You are home, home within My heart.

- My child, be still and know that you are within My heart.

- Love is who you are.

- Within My heart you will be forever.

- From My heart you bring love and light to the world.

- Be that which you truly are.

- You are in Me and I am in you.

- Allow My love and light to be for you not a wish, not a hope, not even a leap of faith, but a knowing deep within your own heart.

- My child, My love and your love, My heart and your heart, are one. Live within My heart.

- **God is reaching out to you. Reach back!**

Remember This

You are God's beloved child. You are a spiritual being having an earthly experience. God speaks to you through the Bible, historic religion, people, nature, and the love that is your essence. Jesus, God with us, illumines the truth about your divine identity. Jesus, through his words and actions, demonstrates God's divine intent for your life, and all our lives. By discerning God's loving voice within the Bible, and the transforming reality established by Jesus, your Spiritual Dawn emerges before you. As you claim fully your spiritual identity, your fear diminishes, your vision clears, peace descends upon your heart, and joy, gratitude and grace radiate within you and from you. By embracing your life journey as fundamentally spiritual, and seeking renewed connection with the source of your life and all life, your Spiritual Dawn will culminate within the very Heart of God—Home.

CHAPTER 7

Awakening to Life In and From the Heart of God

Through the years as a pastor I remember stating that the love of Christ is within each one of us, that each of us has access to Christ's love, and that we can choose to live from that love or not. While that may be a helpful image to internalize and integrate into our daily life, it is only a part of the truth. While on the one hand we like to think of God as all-powerful, we prefer that God not be all powerful over us. We treasure our free will and independence. **It is one thing to have God's love within us, and quite another to reside within God's love completely.**

With God's love within you, you can make that love the defining quality of everything you say and do, or of some things, some people, some situations, or of no one and under no circumstances. Journeying now into your Spiritual Dawn, you are awakening in a totally new place and consciousness. You are awakening within the Heart of God, gaining a profoundly different perspective. Imagine seeing with God's eyes, hearing with God's ears, touching with God's hands, loving with God's heart.

Tomorrow the world around you will be the same as today. The thoughts within your mind have provided a running commentary of assessment, judgment, affirmation and condemnation, and will continue flowing unsolicited in your mind, until you experience an awakening of your innermost being. The world around you has not changed. You are awakening from an unconscious state where you were consumed by the material world. Remember, you are a spiritual being, having an earthly experience. When fear alters your love, remember that you can reject your fear and choose love. Remembering and knowing who you truly are, you can make a new choice. You can choose to remain in the world asleep or stay in the world fully awake to divine truth.

Fully awake, you will choose to live each day, each moment in and from the Heart of God. You will **see** from the Heart of God the beauty of every living thing. You will see through to the heart, the love, of every person you encounter, family, friends, strangers. You will **listen** from the Heart of God. You will recognize joy, gratitude, compassion and love. You will recognize fear, sorrow, doubt and pain. You will **reach out to others** from the Heart of God. You will reach out and extend your hand with healing love, comforting embrace, forgiveness and grace, consciously residing within God's heart. You will **love** from the Heart of God. You will be who you truly are: child of God, created in love to be love, to bring healing, wholeness, peace and joy to every child of God.

You are of God! You are God's light in the world! Stay awake! Live your life in and from the heart of God!

Story: Be Your True Self

No one could believe that Jane and Mary were sisters. Mary would bound out of bed energized, ready to take on the world, full of excitement. Jane on the other hand frequently pulled the covers up over her head in hopes of fending off the morning. Mary wasn't exactly quiet in the morning, either. Jane referred to her as more annoying at 7:00 a.m. than a whole barnyard full of competing roosters. Jane got out of bed when she was good and ready, and spoke only when spoken to.

In elementary school, one of their teachers noted to the principal, that the girls were about as different as they come. On the playground, Jane could be found predictably on the bench closest to the classroom, waiting for the bell to ring so she could get back in class and get the day over with. Now Mary was another matter. Mary might be anywhere. The only thing you could be certain of was that she would be in motion with her eyes wide and her mouth moving. Hand Mary a blank piece of paper and her face would light up as the wheels of creativity began to turn. Hand a blank piece of paper to Jane and her face would reflect the page. Blank. Isn't it amazing how different two people can be?

If you asked Jane how she was, she'd say, "Okay". Mary's response to the same question? "Great!" Ask Jane what her favorite holiday was, and she would answer, "The day after any holiday." Ask Mary? "Must I choose just one?" Send the two out the door and upon their return ask what they had seen. Mary saw butterflies, flowers, blue sky, Mrs. Olson, and three ants on the mailbox. Jane saw an old car in front of the house and the same things that were there the day before. Jane and Mary actually saw and experienced many of the same things much of their lives, but they viewed them very differently.

Jane was devastated when Mary died suddenly at age sixty. She was inconsolable. At Mary's funeral one person after another shared wonderful, joy-filled memories about Mary. Jane could only listen, receiving each remembrance with a great sense of loss and intense pain. Jane fell into a deep depression. An old friend sent her a letter of encouragement and suggested that she write a letter to Mary. This is that letter:

Mary, when you died, I was angrier than I have ever been and you know how angry I can be over very little events. It took a long time before I realized that the level of my anger was equal to the level of my pain. In fact, that my anger was my pain, my fear turned outward. Losing you was like losing the only acceptable part of myself. Everybody loved you. I know many only tolerated me because I was your sister.

You remember how you used to tease me about not ever looking in the mirror, how I would always wear a hat so I could avoid fixing my hair in front of a mirror? You always told me I was pretty. Thanks for that, but that wasn't why I couldn't bear looking into the mirror. I had turned into such a negative, anti-social person that I was actually afraid of what I would see. It didn't help that I had a terrible dream one Sunday night after hearing the story Jesus told about the land owner who sent his servant out to collect the profits and the first two were beaten, and the last, the land owner's son, they killed. I dreamt I saw the face of the one who killed him, and it was mine! Then I dreamt that I got out of bed and looked in the mirror and saw myself bending over Jesus, who was lying on the ground. And as I moved around to the side, I saw that I was hammering a nail through his hand into the wooden cross. I still cannot look in a mirror, for fear of what I will see.

In you, I always saw the goodness, the gentleness, the joy, and the unconditional love of Jesus. I so feared I was not as loving as you that I decided never to try. I was miserable. I tried to make you miserable too, and I know I have been successful in making many other people in my life miserable. I feel that I need you now more than ever, and you are gone. I've done what you would do. I have prayed about it every day, and I think for maybe the first time, I have stopped my negative thoughts long enough to actually hear God's voice. I'm going to do everything I can do to be more like you, one day at a time.

I love you forever. Watch over me. Love, Jane, your grumpy sister.

Jane put the letter in an envelope, placed it in the mailbox and raised the little red flag. A couple days later, Jane went to get her mail, and to her amazement there was an envelope with just her first name on it. She hurried into the house and opened the letter. There were just a few words on it, but Jane's heart began to pound. The letter was signed, "With my love always, Mary." This is what the letter said:

Jane, thanks for the letter. I love you so much. Remember this: you have as much love, goodness, gentleness and joy within you as I ever had. And my goodness, dear sister, don't try to be like me. Do what I always did. Strive to be more like Jesus/God who has created us all in love. Write me again. I love hearing from you. Love always, Mary.

From that very day, Jane's life began to change, really change. Day by day she would write a letter to Mary, and a day or two later there would be a letter from Mary for Jane in the mailbox. The letters from Mary began to have a profound impact on Jane's daily life. The looks Jane began to get from people she had known her whole life began to change as Jane herself changed. Once close friends of Mary now began to invite this newly revised edition of Jane to dinner, the theater and family gatherings.

It was twelve years after Mary's death that Jane gathered enough courage to actually study herself in the mirror. At first she saw only an aging face, framed with very white hair, but then what she saw took her breath away. In the mirror, as though she were looking through a window, a scene began to appear. She gasped as she saw a scene from a long-ago time. A crowd was standing along a dusty road, some people taunting, some people weeping. Then she saw him so close she saw the sweat mingled with blood on his brow. It was Jesus and he was carrying the heavy wooden cross upon which he was about to die. A woman stepped out from the crowd and lovingly gave him a cup of cool water. He looked into her eyes with love and gratitude for her act of compassion. As the woman turned, Jane was able to see her face. It was Jane's face!

Jane's eyes overflowed with tears of joy. She knew that she had become the woman she had longed to be, a woman gentle, compassionate and loving. Jane had become like the sister she loved so deeply and admired so completely.

That very night, at seventy-eight years of age, Jane passed from this life to the next, to the loving arms of God. Following Jane's funeral, the pastor was handed a note and a key that Jane had left with her will. The key was to a post office box that Jane had had since Mary's death. There the pastor found all the letters that Jane had sent to Mary, and a request of the pastor. "Please combine these letters with those you will find in my bottom desk drawer and give them to my nephew to share with the generations to come. I pray they may learn from me what took me most of my lifetime to understand. Choose to live each moment of your life from within the Heart of God. There you will experience love, joy and peace that is beyond words to describe, and you will always see a beautiful reflection in the mirror."

You see, Jane had gone out after dark each night after sending a letter to Mary and had left a response that she knew would be like her sister's own words. God's voice, the voice of love, affirmation and hope through Jane's own hand.

What are you waiting for? Choose to live fully awake. Welcome the expansion of your own Spiritual Dawn. It is time to return home to life in and from the Heart of God!

Spiritual Pause (minimum of 10 minutes)

Through the eyes of your heart:

- Look to the sky. Imagine a spot of light.

- Stay focused on that spot of light.

- The light is slowly expanding.

- As the light expands it becomes more intense, brighter than anything you have ever seen. You are transfixed in awe.

- The light fills the sky and now the light draws near and envelopes you completely.

- Tears run down your cheeks. You have never felt such love.

- Stay present. Allow the love to fill you.

- You have entered into the Heart of God. You are Home!

From within the Heart of God,

- You now see from the Heart of God.

- You now listen from the Heart of God.

- You now reach out to others from the Heart of God.

- You now love from the Heart of God.

In the Heart of God you are your truest self. This is the day of your awakening, the day of new life. Be still and know.

Remember This

God's love is within you. Make that love the defining quality of everything you say and do. Journey into your Spiritual Dawn and onward into the very Heart of God. The people and the world around you may appear unchanged, but you, awakened child of God, are changed forever. Fully awake, make a conscious choice to live each day, every moment, in and from the Heart of God. One day, one moment, one encounter at a time, you now see from the Heart of God, listen and hear from the Heart of God, respond to every situation and person from the Heart of God. From the Heart of God, you become one with God's love as you extend your hand with healing touch, comforting embrace, forgiveness and grace. From God's heart, God's love shines to you and through you to the world.

Stay awake! Stay awake!

CONCLUSION

Thoughts for the Journey

- Chapter 1: God's Love Within You

- Chapter 2: Interpreting the Bible

- Chapter 3: God's Rule Book

- Chapter 4: Jesus in the Room

- Chapter 5: Faith

- Chapter 6: True Identity

- Chapter 7: Salt and Light

Conclusion

- Daily Affirmation

- Thoughts for the Journey

- Remember This (Summary)

- Living In and From the Heart of God—Practical Tools for Staying Awake
- Glossary
- About the Author
- Salt and Light in My Life

MY DAILY AFFIRMATION

Today I choose to live Awake!

I am God's beloved child.

I will live each moment of this day
from within the Heart of God.

I will see from the Heart of God.

I will listen from the Heart of God.

I will reach out to others from the Heart of God.

I will love from the Heart of God.

GOD IS LOVE.

When I am loving, I am in the Heart of God
and God is within me.

I AM HOME.

THOUGHTS FOR THE JOURNEY

Chapter 1: God's Love Within You

John 17:20-26 (NRSV)

(Jesus said)*I ask not only on behalf of these, but also on behalf of those who will believe in me through their word, that they may all be one. As you, Father, are in me and I am in you, may they also be in us, so that the world may believe that you have sent me. The glory that you have given me I have given them, so that they may be one, as we are one, I in them and you in me, that they may become completely one, so that the world may know that you have sent me and have loved them even as you have loved me. Father, I desire that those also, whom you have given me, may be with me where I am, to see my glory, which you have given me because you loved me before the foundation of the world. Righteous Father, the world does not know you, but I know you; and these know that you have sent me. I made your name known to them, and I will make it known, so that the love with which you have loved me may be in them, and I in them.*

Are we truly one with God? Are we one with one another? We are truly one with God, but we don't really believe it. If we try to make our way in this life on our own, we will never be one with others because our fears are too great.

Jesus knows that if we are to experience life as God intends, if we are to fulfill divine purpose in the course of our earthly lives, we must know and believe that we are one with God. And as Jesus prays: "I made your name known to them, and I will make it known, so that the love with which you have loved me may be in them and I in them" (John 17:26) If you knew every moment that the full power of God's love is within you, would you be likely to respond differently to the events and encounters of your day? You know, the basics:

- You are late for work or an appointment and just as you get to the intersection an elderly person begins to slowly shuffle across in front of you. The light turns green and she's just now made it to the middle of your hood. **The power of God's love is within you.** Do you honk? Do you holler? Do you smile and mouth, "It's okay"?

- You have a long list of tasks to accomplish in a limited amount of time, and you have planned about twenty minutes to deliver some items to a senior family member you help out regularly. You arrive and are met with a list of needs that the individual expects you to take care of now, with no sensitivity to the fact that you have a very busy life and much to do. **The power of God's love is within you.** Do you sigh with exasperation and dictate your list, or...?

- There is someone of an ethnic origin different from your own in front of you in the grocery line. First he has difficulty understanding what the clerk is saying because his English is very limited. Then when he goes to pay he is a few dollars short of the total bill. **The power of God's love is within you.** What will your reaction be? What are the thoughts of your mind, your body language, the expression on your face, the feeling in your gut? Will you say anything, do anything, comment to the clerk after he has left?

When we grasp the truth of God's love within us, we gain courage and may respond differently to many situations.

The coat of arms of the Netherlands illustrates what it means to be one with God and to be connected to God's love. It shows two clasped hands, one descending from above and the other reaching up from below. The motto on the coat of arms is, "God Wills; I Can". As committed followers of Christ, I think an addition to that image may be helpful for us as we strive to be people who live conscious of the power of God's love within us. Imagine the hand from above grasping your hand, and your other hand extended to another to pass on the power of God's love. Too often we have grasped the hand of God and selectively placed our other hand in our pocket.

You know when you are connected to the power of God's love, and when that connection translates to loving thoughts, words and actions toward the greatest and the least in God's world. When we are connected and we pass it on, it feels wonderful!

On the ceiling of the Sistine Chapel in Rome, Michael Angelo painted a powerful image which communicates God's desire to be connected to each of us. The painting depicts Almighty God, high in the heavens, reaching down to touch the hand of Adam, whose body is also reaching up to touch the hand of God. When we find our thoughts, words and actions are no longer coming from the limitless store of love within us, we need to see this image in our minds and reach back to Almighty God and grasp that extended hand.

God never lets go! When fear and frustration control our thoughts, words and actions, we have let go of the hand of God and entered into our personal wilderness where hope fades, courage wanes and ego reigns, and it leads nowhere. Grasp God's hand and never let go. I promise, God's hand will never move. **The power of God's love is within you**. I see it! When we grasp one another's hands, we are one, all children of God. Amen.

Chapter 2: Interpreting the Bible

Mark 10:13-16 (RSV)

And they were bringing children to Jesus, that he might touch them; and the disciples rebuked them. But when Jesus saw it he was indignant, and said to them, "Let the children come to me, do not hinder them; for to such belongs the kingdom of God. Truly, I say to you, whoever does not receive the kingdom of God like a child shall not inherit it." And he took them in his arms and blessed them, laying his hands upon them.

The most inspiring, poignant interpreter I ever met was an eight-year old. During Sunday worship, at the point of my talk with the children I said, "I have a few questions about the Bible." Before I could continue, Joseph proceeded to answer. "God made the world and every living thing. God put us in charge of taking care of everything and all the people. We didn't do a very good job, so God gave Moses ten rules to help us get on track. We don't like rules, so we did what we wanted to do and most people ignored God.

"God didn't give up. He sent prophets to straighten us out, and we ignored them, too. God gave up on that plan and decided to send his Son Jesus to show us how to live God's way. Some people liked Jesus, but some thought loving everyone was too nice. Jesus loved us so much he didn't give up. He kept loving God's way, no matter what.

"The guys in power thought Jesus was a trouble maker, so they got the governor to kill him on a cross. Jesus died. It was very sad, but it ended happy because Jesus didn't stay dead. Jesus came back to life. Now we don't have to be afraid because Jesus died for us. God isn't mad at us anymore and when we die, we will come back to life in heaven. That's where God lives and it is the coolest place in the whole Milky Way galaxy.

"After Jesus came back to life and went to heaven, those people who believed Jesus knew the best way to be, helped everyone else understand that God's way is love and that it is the best power."

I didn't ask any more questions, I just said, "Amen." The whole congregation broke into applause. Indeed, through the minds and hearts of children, God often speaks most clearly. Amen.

Chapter 3: God's Rule Book

Luke 13:10-17 (NRSV):

Now Jesus was teaching in one of the synagogues on the Sabbath. And just then there appeared a woman with a spirit that had crippled her for eighteen years. She was bent over and was quite unable to stand up straight. When Jesus saw her, he called her over and said, "Woman, you are set free from your ailment." When he laid his hands on her, immediately she stood up straight and began praising God. But the leader of the synagogue, indignant because Jesus had cured on the Sabbath, kept saying to the crowd, "There are six days on which work ought to be done; come on those days and be cured, and not on the Sabbath day." But the Lord answered him and said, "You hypocrites! Does not each of you on the Sabbath untie his ox or his donkey from the manger, and lead it away to give it water? And ought not this woman, a daughter of Abraham whom Satan bound for eighteen long years, be set free from this bondage on the Sabbath day?" When he said this, all his opponents were put to shame; and the entire crowd was rejoicing at all the wonderful things that he was doing.

The Church certainly is not perfect. It wasn't in the time of Jesus and it certainly isn't now. You have probably heard it said that there is only one thing wrong with the church—it's full of people!

The church of which Jesus spoke was enmeshed in rules. Amazing how ten rules became hundreds. The Sabbath was a strict day of rest, man's interpretation of God's command. Certain foods were deemed unclean. Women were not allowed to speak to men in public. A woman caught in the act of adultery was to be stoned to death. Upon the death of a husband, a woman became the property of her husband's eldest brother. The leaders of the church believed they were maintaining good order by preserving ancient laws and codes.

We look at the actions of the religious leaders of that day and find them narrow-minded and missing the point of God's true intent for humanity. We are much more advanced. If it is Sunday and we see someone in need, we simply respond, don't we? We may not be narrow-minded based upon our religious beliefs, but we can be just as pedantic as the leaders of the synagogue.

Meet Henry: "I believe in helping those who help themselves. Pull yourselves up by your bootstraps—that's the way I made it. If you don't have insurance, there must be a reason. Just because you live here doesn't mean you are entitled to it."

Meet Ethel: "I have new neighbors. I can't even pronounce their names. I can hear them chatting in the back yard, but I can't understand a word they say. One of them came to the door the other day and I pretended I wasn't home. You can't be too careful these days."

Meet Max: "I saw the saddest thing the other day. There was a woman trying to cross the street, but she was so bent over I was sure she was going to be hit because she couldn't lift her head to see anything above her shoelaces. I held my breath until she was safely on the other side of the street. What a stressor!"

Do you recognize any of these people? At least one of them is a member of my family. We insulate ourselves so from one another that we are sometimes what I call AWOL Christians. We are in when it's comfortable, and out when it's not. Full-time Christians follow Jesus' example all the time, when it's easy and when it's hard. Good old Henry believes in helping those who help themselves. Do we believe God offers conditional assistance? Pulling yourself up by your own bootstraps is fine, assuming everyone has boots. Ethel is so fearful that she won't even open the door. For her, difference is to be feared. We miss great richness when we only connect with those just like us. Max was pathetic. Help the woman across the street!

For us, it's all about fear—fear of being taken advantage of, fear that our share of the pie will be reduced, fear of discomfort, fear of difference, fear of newness, fear that assisting will put us in jeopardy. Jesus did not so much as pause before healing the woman bent over for eighteen years. He didn't know her name, her ancestry, her family, her beliefs, her resources, her marital status, her economic status, her citizenship. He just saw a woman with an obvious need, and he met that need with unflinching love and acceptance. God's rule book is very brief—ten commands to follow and a promise of eternal joy. How hard can it be? Love God above all else, and your neighbor as yourself.

Remember Jesus' answer to the question, "…and who is my neighbor?" Jesus told a story of a man, a foreigner, going down to Jericho, who fell among robbers. The robbers left the man beaten and near death. A priest came by and saw the man, but passed him by. A Levite, a temple leader, also came to the place, saw the man and passed by on the other side. Then a Samaritan, despised within the Jewish community, came by, saw the injured man and had compassion for him. The Samaritan stopped, bound up the man's wounds, then placed him on his own animal and brought him to an inn where he cared for him. The next day he paid the innkeeper to continue to care for the man until he was well.

This story is a powerful example of God's intent for humanity, and also an excellent example of what God endeavors to illumine within the whole of the Bible. What we call the Ten Commandments (the promises between God and his creation), and this parable (story) told by Jesus, are perfect examples of the Bible as the Living Word of God—intended to guide us back to our true identity, back to God.

Continue your journey with open hands and open hearts. Amen.

Chapter 4: Jesus In the Room

Luke 23:33-43 (NRSV):

When they came to the place that is called The Skull, they crucified Jesus there with the criminals, one on his right and one on his left. Then Jesus said, "Father, forgive them; for they do not know what they are doing." And they cast lots to divide his clothing. And the people stood by, watching; but the leaders scoffed at him, saying, "He saved others; let him save himself if he is the Messiah of God, his chosen one!" The soldiers also mocked him, coming up and offering him sour wine, and saying, "If you are the King of the Jews, save yourself!" There was also an inscription over him, "This is the King of the Jews." One of the criminals who were hanged there kept deriding him and saying, "Are you not the Messiah? Save yourself and us!" But the other rebuked him, saying, "Do you not fear God, since you are under the same sentence of condemnation? And we indeed have been condemned justly, for we are getting what we deserve for our deeds, but this man has done nothing wrong." Then he said, "Jesus, remember me when you come into your kingdom." He replied, "Truly I tell you, today you will be with me in Paradise."

Does the reality of Jesus' identity make any difference in your life? If we truly understand what Jesus teaches and lives, it changes everything. It changes us from the inside out! What are you like when:

- You are relaxed and calm?

- You are under stress?

- You are in pain or sick?

- You are extremely busy?

- You are tired?

- You are stressed, in pain, busy, tired, and someone very close to you asks you to do something?

Now let's assume you are at home and Jesus is in the room. Now what are you like when:

- You are relaxed and calm with Jesus in the room?

- You are under stress and Jesus is in the room?

- You are in pain or sick and Jesus is in the room?

- You are extremely busy and Jesus is in the room?

- You are tired and Jesus is in the room?

- You are stressed, in pain, busy and tired and Jesus is in the room?

You are different, aren't you? Does Jesus' literal presence make you a better person? It does, doesn't it? **When Jesus is present, love overpowers all negative energy and impulse.** Might the thought of Jesus' literal presence change how you react under other than optimum conditions, even at work, on the road, at the market, the gas station, at school? Even when an officer pulls you over for speeding, an old woman cuts in front of you on the freeway, or you are in conversation with someone who has very different political views than yours? Might the thought of Jesus' presence impact your patience and grace in every situation that you can think of? It should! It should because Jesus is in the room, he is always present, and we have access to loving response always!

Take care of yourself!

- Get the rest you need.

- Counter your stress with whatever calms you: exercise, a good book, listening to music, driving a few golf balls.

- When you are sick or in pain, take time to heal.

- When you are really busy, give energy to those things which are truly important.

- Remember to pray, take a deep breath, and allow Jesus to walk with you.

Jesus is in the room. Before you contort your face, cop a tone or say a caustic word, remember that Jesus is in the room. And Jesus changes everything! Amen.

Chapter 5: Faith

Luke 21:5-19 (NRSV):

When some were speaking about the temple, how it was adorned with beautiful stones and gifts dedicated to God, Jesus said, "As for these things that you see, the days will come when not one stone will be left upon another; all will be thrown down." They asked him, "Teacher, when will this be, and what will be the sign that this is about to take place?" And he said, "Beware that you are not led astray; for many will come in my name and say, 'I am he!' and, 'The time is near!' Do not go after them. When you hear of wars and insurrections, do not be terrified; for these things must take place first, but the end will not follow immediately." Then he said to them, "Nation will rise against nation, and kingdom against kingdom; there will be great earthquakes, and in various places famines and plagues; and there will be dreadful portents and great signs from heaven. But before all this occurs, they will arrest you and persecute you; they will hand you over to synagogues and prisons, and you will be brought before kings and governors because of my name. This will give you an opportunity to testify. So make up your minds not to prepare your defense in advance; for I will give you words and a wisdom that none of your opponents will be able to withstand or contradict. You will be betrayed even by parents and brothers, by relatives and friends; and they will put some of you to death. You will be hated by all because of my name. But not a hair of your head will perish. By your endurance you will gain your souls."

Faith! Is that all we have to do, say we have faith? Nothing else is required? Just believe and the gifts of heaven will fall into our laps? Faith is a verb, an action word! To say we believe only illumines the pathway before us. Saying we believe is not faith. Being baptized says nothing of faith. In baptism God enters into our lives and claims us in love forever. Our response is ours to initiate. We can choose to take the gift and do nothing with it. What a waste!

Faith inspires loving action. The opposite of faith is fear and worry. When fear and worry are dominant within us, then fear and worry contribute to the words we speak and impose the creation of boundaries to acts of love and kindness. As we ponder the depth of our own faith, it is important for us to acknowledge that as people of faith we stand in the shadow of giants.

Think of the faith of Moses, an infant set adrift down the Nile River, rescued out of the water by Pharaoh's daughter, raised in the house of the pharaoh. Moses became aware of his true identity as the son of Hebrew slaves and, hearing God's voice, answered by turning away from his privileged life in order to fulfill God's call to rescue the people of Israel, held captive in Egypt. Faith takes action! What a story. In an effort to fulfill God's plan, Moses and the people spend forty years searching for the Promised Land. Who would you follow who got you lost even twice? How does our faith appear in the shadow of Moses?

Jesus embodies faith that never waivers. Jesus, a carpenter's son, grows up in a small village. He is raised in the Torah and lives its teachings. He is neither passive nor resigned. Jesus grows in knowledge, and is alive in faith. So certain is Jesus of his purpose and God's intent for the world that he suffers insult, threats, accusations of hypocrisy and hierarchy, and is ultimately beaten at the hands of Roman soldiers at the insistence of the religious leaders of his faith, and suffers an excruciating death on a cross. How does our faith reflect in the shadow of Jesus?

Saul, a zealous Jew, was a persecutor of Jesus, arresting, imprisoning and executing the early Christians. Saul changes only after a terrifying encounter on the road to Damascus—an encounter with the resurrected Jesus. "Saul", Jesus says, "why do you persecute me?" Saul's world is turned upside down. Jesus is alive. Jesus is the Savior of the world. Saul, now named Paul by Jesus, makes a dramatic conversion, turns from his hate-filled accusations of those who preach Christ, and becomes Christ's ambassador to the Gentiles, the non-Jews. Paul's faith came alive in Christ. Paul is outcast, tortured and imprisoned, ultimately dying in captivity. How does our faith stand up in the shadow of Paul?

1,400 years after Paul, a Catholic monk named Martin Luther turned the church upside down. Risking his life, he refused to recant, resolute that God, revealed to us in Jesus Christ, was a gracious God, merciful and accessible to everyone. Luther translated the Bible from Hebrew and Greek into the language of his German people. For the first time the Word of God was accessible to common man. Standing before the hierarchy of the church, facing excommunication and possible death, Luther stood firm, stating, "Here I stand; I cannot be moved." With those words the Christian Reformation took flight. The grace-filled gospel of Jesus Christ which we proclaim was revealed through the living faith of a single man by the name of Luther. How does our faith stand up in the shadow of Martin?

About now, I suspect you are feeling a bit faint-hearted about your faith. Your faith is a gift. The seeds of faith are planted within each of us. Faith is a verb, an action word. Only you know whether your faith is passive or active, seldom spoken or spoken and lifted daily. Each of us can grow in our faith, every day of our lives, if we have the will and make the commitment. Our faith is indeed lived out in the shadow of giants, but you are the one through whom your family and all whose lives you touch will be inspired to nurture and live out their faith.

Your faithfulness inspires my faith. You have a contribution to make to God's gracious, loving kingdom. Do not die with your faith a dormant seed. Don't die with one word of gratitude still on your lips, or one intended loving act unshared. Your faith nurtured, your faith lived out in loving action, will empower you and empower the faith within others. To live by faith is to put love into action, every moment of every day, without fear of any kind. That kind of faith is within you. Choose to live your faith and you will live from love. Amen.

Chapter 6: True Identity

Mark 9:2-9 (NRSV):

Six days later, Jesus took with him Peter and James and John, and led them up a high mountain apart, by themselves. And he was transfigured before them, and his clothes became dazzling white, such as no one on earth could bleach them. And there appeared to them Elijah with Moses, who were talking with Jesus. Then Peter said to Jesus, "Rabbi, it is good for us to be here; let us make three dwellings, one for you, one for Moses, and one for Elijah." He did not know what to say, for they were terrified. Then a cloud overshadowed them, and from the cloud there came a voice, "This is my Son, the Beloved; listen to him!" Suddenly when they looked around, they saw no one with them any more, but only Jesus. As they were coming down the mountain, he ordered them to tell no one about what they had seen, until after the Son of Man had risen from the dead.

On a mountainside far removed from the crowds who sought to be in his presence, Jesus rested with his trusted disciples Peter, James and John. Before them, Jesus was transfigured, bathed in light from heaven. Then appeared Elijah with Moses, the two great patriarchs of the faith. A cloud overshadowed them and from the cloud came a voice: "This is my Son, the beloved. Listen to him." And suddenly they were alone with Jesus, their lives forever changed. Peter, James and John were now witnesses to the true identity of Jesus! The kingdom of God is at hand; God entered into human history in the person of Jesus of Nazareth. Jesus is the Son of God, Immanuel, God with us!

Through the witness of Peter, James and John, we too are recipients of divine truth. We know the true identity of Jesus. Ultimately God shows us how it all turns out in resurrection and new creation, so that we recognize transfigurations when they take place in the midst of the sometimes chaotic confusion of our own lives. Knowing how it ultimately turns out enables us to endure and transcend when the harsh realities of human life, hardship and heartache overshadow us. We are able to survive the harsh realities solely because we cling to God's promises. We become able to transcend what at first may seem impossible to endure, because our faith renews our love, and our love creates new life and hope.

This is the power of divine love which surpasses all human understanding. Only in experiencing divine love are we able to recognize transfigurations when they take place in our own lives and in the lives of others. We hear and say things like, "Boy, that was lucky!" or "Wasn't that a coincidence, that was an amazing turn of events, isn't it amazing how time heals all wounds." Give me a break! Luck, coincidence, fluke, amazing turns of events, time healing all, represent our feeble attempts to explain what we don't fully understand or believe.

God is here! God is everywhere! God does not control our choices, we make our own. We make good choices and we make bad ones. Often when we least expect it, God enters in and transfigures, brings light and new life to what may appear to be hopeless or unchangeable. **Nothing in your life is unchangeable, unless you have decided that it is.** We come to the conclusion of hopelessness all the time. We give up on ourselves and we give others power over us. We fear the hard work of changing ourselves. We grow weary of the struggle, and we resign to simply endure.

Is your God dead? Do you believe what you profess about dying daily to sin and, through the gift of Christ, rising each day to new life with limitless possibility? My life isn't about me. Your life is not about you! Your life is a precious gift from Almighty God. You are born to share the love within you fully, so that the love of God will be the sole motivating force in our world, among all people.

Christ has freed you to become a co-creator with God in the emergence of the Kingdom of God here on earth. Jesus comes to demonstrate the Heart of God. God is made visible through Jesus in every act of compassion, kindness, forgiveness and grace. Jesus' true identity is undeniable. He is Immanuel, God with us! When you forget who you are, your true identity becomes clouded by your fears, the voices of family and friends, and your experience as a human being. But your bad memory does not negate the truth.

You are a redeemed child of Almighty God. Through the gift of Christ you have been forgiven and set free—yesterday, today, tomorrow, and for all your tomorrows. Through Christ you are empowered to amend your life and make the difficult changes that you need to make, in order to give the gift of you, following Christ's example.

If you had been the winner of a mega lottery, would you continue to live off your present income and hide the rest of it? Of course not! Your mind would be reeling with the possibilities of what you could do with it. Well, my friend in Christ, you have won more than the lottery! You have been claimed and empowered by Almighty God! There is no limit to what you can contribute to the world in which you live. Every loving word you speak, and every loving thing you do gives life to others. Do not let your life come to an end, do not die with one single loving word unspoken or one single act of love unshared.

What words of love, what acts of love will you give away today? Christ has empowered you to be a giver of love—only love! Be who you truly are, one day, one encounter at a time. Enter your Spiritual Dawn! Amen.

Chapter 7: Salt and Light

Matthew 5:13-14 (NRSV):

(Jesus said) *You are the salt of the earth; but if salt has lost its taste, how can its saltiness be restored? It is no longer good for anything, but is thrown out and trampled under foot. You are the light of the world. A city built on a hill cannot be hid.*

You are the salt of the earth! You are the light of the world! Picture in your mind a crowd gathering as they watch Jesus approach. Jesus is very aware of their presence. He sees them with his eyes and he sees them with his heart. In order for all to be able to see and hear him, Jesus heads for higher ground and the crowd follows. Jesus sits down and looks the crowd over. He sees people who have known hardship and joy. Most have known want, a few have known plenty. Some are hungry, some are sick, some have come with family or friends, some have come alone. Jesus has not attracted a singular category of people, the rich or poor, the illiterate or the educated, the powerful or the powerless, Jews or gentiles. They are all there. Jesus, seeing with his heart into each individual heart, sees the children of God, period.

Jesus is, however, with them for a specific purpose—to remind them of who they are! They are the salt of the earth and the light of the world! Jesus calls them to be who they truly are. Jesus' single desire is to awaken them to their true identity, so they can do something that will change the world. He calls them to live their lives in and from the Heart of God!

Are you expecting Jesus to speak to you directly? I hope so, because that is exactly what he is going to do.

- Jesus sees you, really sees YOU.

- Jesus knows everything, everything about you.

- Jesus sees your heart.

- You are God's beloved child, period.

You may consider this good news or disappointing news, but God doesn't care about the stuff of your life, only the love in your life! God cares about the love in your life, and that you find your way back to the truth that love is all that you are. Everything else is temporary, finite. Jesus stands before you, looks into your eyes, your eyes, and says to you, "You are the salt of the earth. You are the light of the world."

What is the voice in your head saying right now? Please find someone else, or:

- I'm generous and kind when I feel like it.

- I've done some unkind things in my past.

- I've hurt people, disappointed people.

- I have no intention of forgiving everyone.

- I'm better at rubbing salt into someone's wound than being an uplifting spirit.

- I doubt that those who know me best would call me the light of the world.

Welcome to the human race!

The world is a noisy place, as are the voices in our heads. Our thoughts often drown out the truth. By your very existence you are equipped and called to be the salt of the earth and light of the world. One thing is needed—that you commit to being that which you are. How? By living your daily life in and from the Heart of God. Even if you in your human state know instinctively what is required to love as God does, it is not a matter of faith alone, but a matter of inner knowing, daily owning your identity. In so doing:

- You will be the salt which enhances all that is, for the good of all.

- You will be the light of the world, which brings clarity of vision and purpose into your daily life, and which will expand to help bring clarity of vision and purpose into more lives than you can ever imagine.

How? In your love, God is present, all powerful, and the world is changed!

I invite you to fold your hands, bow your head, and slowly read and experience the words that follow. As you breathe in, the air that enters your lungs is absorbed into your bloodstream and gives life to every cell of your body. God is within each breath. Your life, here, now, is a gift of God. God fills you with each breath; that life-giving gift is love. It is only the fearful thoughts of your mind that cause you to live with restraint. There is nothing to fear. You have belonged to God since the beginning of time. You belong to God now, and in Christ, you shall forever.

Breathe deeply. You are the salt of the earth and the light of the world. Believe it! Live daily in and from the Heart of God. Amen.

Remember This

Chapter 1

You are a spiritual being having a human experience. You have come from God and you will return to God's loving presence. Living from your spiritual essence (love), your life has no limits and you become a healing light in this world.

Chapter 2

The Bible is a gift. Within the Bible is a record of God's presence throughout time. Reading and studying through the words and teachings of Jesus, you understand that God is loving and gracious. Most importantly, you are reminded of God's love for all people. The Bible awakens you to the truth of who you are, whose you are, and what you are to be about on this earth.

Chapter 3

The holy writings available to Jesus primarily included what we know as the first five books of the Old Testament of the Bible, writings of the prophets and stories. Jesus in his teaching clarified and expanded upon God's will and divine intent. The sacred writings were the foundation of Jesus' teaching and represented the history of Israel. The Messiah, the Savior, was expected to redeem Israel. Jesus fulfills God's divine intent, not only for Israel, but for the whole human family.

Chapter 4

Jesus is the Savior of the world. As you make this earthly journey, Jesus (Immanuel, God with us) provides a path upon which every human being is invited to travel. Jesus Christ cannot be contained within institutional creeds, doctrines, traditions, rites, worship practices, or selective ethnic or cultural origins. Christ is bigger than that. The Christ, the Savior of the world, the way home, exists asleep or awake within you. Christ, God incarnate, the creator of all, exists within Christians and—hold onto your hats—within every human heart.

It is not the "correct" belief that saves you, but faith (knowing) that God's all-powerful love and loving intent for you and all humanity is fully revealed in Jesus Christ.

Jesus changes everything!

Chapter 5

God continues to create and participate in your world and in your individual life, day by day, by day. Birth and death are physical realities you understand. Where you were before birth, and where you will be after your physical death remains uncertain, except by faith. In the midst of your life, you forget who you truly are. Awakening to the vast dimensions and presence of God, your faith becomes relevant, an unobstructed pathway to life in and from the Heart of God and your own personal Spiritual Dawn.

- God is the creator of all life.

- God's divine intent is that all humanity live from love, respecting self and others.

- You have come from God and you will return to God. That is a promise.

- You are to love others as God loves you.

- There is nothing to fear. God is with you in love, always and forever.

Chapter 6

You are God's beloved child. You are a spiritual being having an earthly experience. God speaks to you through the Bible, historic religion, people, nature, and the love that is your essence. Jesus, God with us, illumines the truth about your divine identity. Jesus, through his words and actions, demonstrates God's divine intent for your life, and all our lives. By discerning God's loving voice within the Bible, and the transforming reality established by Jesus, your Spiritual Dawn emerges before you. As you claim fully your spiritual identity, your fear diminishes, your vision clears, peace descends upon your heart, and joy, gratitude and grace radiate within you and from you. By embracing your life journey as fundamentally spiritual, and seeking renewed connection with the source of your life and all life, your Spiritual Dawn will culminate within the very Heart of God—Home.

Chapter 7

God's love is within you. Make that love the defining quality of everything you say and do. Journey into your Spiritual Dawn and onward into the very Heart of God. The people and the world around you may appear unchanged, but you, awakened child of God, are changed forever. Fully awake, make a conscious choice to live each day, every moment, in and from the Heart of God. One day, one moment, one encounter at a time, you now see from the Heart of God, listen and hear from the Heart of God, respond to every situation and person from the Heart of God. From the Heart of God, you become one with God's love as you extend your hand with healing touch, comforting embrace, forgiveness and grace. From God's heart, God's love shines to you and through you to the world.

Stay awake! Stay awake!

LIVING IN AND FROM THE HEART OF GOD

Practical Tools for Staying Awake

What Changes? What will be different when you see every person as God sees them—from only love?

- Family members

- Co-workers

- Friends

- Neighbors

- Strangers

- Social economic groups

- Ethnic groups

- People of other faiths

- Immigrants documented, undocumented
- Foreigners
- Christians
- Jews
- Muslims
- Hindus
- Buddhists
- Atheists
- Agnostics
- Cults
- Tribes

What will be different when you reach out to others from the Heart of God?

- Will you prioritize your time differently?
- Will you engage with more people?
- Will you find your life more fulfilling?
- Will the challenges of your own life seem to be of less importance?

What will be different when you love from the Heart of God?

Create a list:

How will the thoughts of your own mind change?

How will your personal opinions change?

How will your actions change?

How will your daily life change?

How will your most intimate relationships change?

What will you do less?

What will you do more?

How will you continue to nurture and grow spiritually?

A PASTOR'S GLOSSARY

Absolution: forgiveness; formal release from guilt; declaration from a pastor or priest of forgiveness of sins.

Altar: table used as the focus for a religious ritual.

Baptism: a Christian sacrament using water and the words of Christ; official entrance into the Christian family; affirmation as a redeemed child of God and inheritor of eternal life.

Cantor: person who sings solo verses or passages to which the congregation responds.

Chalice: a wine cup used for Holy Communion.

Christian year: begins with Advent (four weeks of preparation for Christ's birth), traces Christ's life, birth through resurrection, followed by 24-27 weeks focusing on Christian living.

Confession: acknowledgement of thoughts, words or actions counter to God's loving intent.

Confirmation: a rite in which a baptized person affirms their Christian faith.

Congregation: members of a specific church.

Covenant code: divine laws.

Creed: a statement of beliefs.

Crucifix: a cross with a figure of Jesus on it.

Divine: of, from or like God.

Divinity: God.

Doctrine: established teaching of principles of religion.

Elements: bread and wine in Holy Communion.

Eucharist: Holy Communion; receiving the consecrated bread and wine representing Christ's body and blood, Christ's sacrificial gift of himself for forgiveness and reconciliation with God.

Forgiveness: process of being forgiving or forgiven.

Gospel: the biblical books which tell the story of the birth, life, death and resurrection of Jesus.

Hell: traditionally described as a spiritual realm of evil and suffering.

Holy Spirit: third person of the trinity (Father, Son and Holy Spirit); three ways God is manifest to humanity.

Hymn: a song of praise to God; formal song sung by the whole congregation.

Immanuel: name for Christ the deliverer; God with us.

Incarnate: embodied in flesh; in human form.

Israelite: member of the ancient Hebrew nation.

Kneel: show reverence and respect; showing submission.

Laity: ordinary people distinct from professionals or experts.

Liturgical: worship with a set form and order.

Liturgy: prescribed form and order of worship.

Lutheran: a church characterized by the theology of Martin Luther.

Martin Luther: theologian; principal figure of the German Reformation who preached the doctrine of justification by faith rather than works.

Ordination: confer holy orders, a ceremony (rite) in which someone is ordained.

Passover: major Jewish festival commemorating the Israelites' liberation from slavery in Egypt.

Pastor: ordained minister in charge of a church or congregation.

Pentateuch: first five books of the Hebrew Bible; the books of Jewish law.

Pentecost: Christian celebration of the gift of the Holy Spirit.

Prayer: a communication with God, offering thanks, requesting guidance, support, healing for self or others.

Priest: ordained Christian minister having authority to perform certain rites and administer certain sacraments.

Prophet: inspired teacher or proclaimer of the will of God.

Protestant: any Christian not belonging to the Roman Catholic or Orthodox Eastern church.

Resurrection: in Christianity, Christ rising from the dead.

Rite: religious ceremony or act.

Sacrament: a rite or practice commanded by Christ utilizing earthly elements; water in baptism, wine and bread in communion.

Sermon: a talk given during a church service based on a passage from the Bible; the proclamation of the Gospel.

Sin: anything we say or do which creates a separation between a person and God.

Stole: a long scarf-like piece of cloth in various colors, often with religious symbols, worn over the shoulders of a pastor or priest.

Ten Commandments: ten divine laws of God.

Theology: the study of the nature of God and religious belief.

Virgin birth: the doctrine of Christ's birth from Mary, who was a virgin.

Wilderness journey: forty-year journey the Israelites traveled in search of the Promised Land.

Worship (Christian): a formal expression of reverence; religious ceremony usually including prayer, scripture reading, sermon by pastor or priest, religious music, singing, sacraments, and religious rites.

About the Author

Rev. Margaret Duttera received her BA in Education and Secondary Teaching Credential from Chico State University in California, and her Masters in Divinity degree from Pacific Lutheran Theological Seminary in Berkeley, California. Margaret taught and coached at Watsonville High School in California from 1971–1978. In 1982 Margaret was ordained and served as Associate Pastor and then Senior Pastor at Lutheran Church of the Cross in Arcadia, California. In 1988 until her retirement in 2008, she served as Senior Pastor at Christ Lutheran Church (Beach Church) in San Clemente, California.

Throughout her pastoral career she has not only empowered and inspired many lives in her faith community, but also as a keynote speaker at several regional events, and as a presenter at the National Assembly of Women of the Evangelical Lutheran Church in America. Margaret was also honored as Pastor of the Year by Women of the Pacific Southwest Synod of the Lutheran Church in America, represented the Evangelical Lutheran Church in America in a segment aired on CBS, and was featured in a piece on the Odyssey Network about "Beach Church" in San Clemente. Throughout the years, she has also been a sought-after speaker at numerous retreats and special events.

Known for her passion to communicate with relevance and humor, Margaret has a special gift for connecting the spiritual with real life. Her personal journey of spiritual growth has ignited a fire within her to awaken forgotten essential roots and to provide a pathway to relevant spirituality for those with little or no foundation, and those who have never experienced the divine truth of their identity.

Salt and Light in My Life

My sister Dee and brother-in-law Dave have always loved me just as I am. Through the years they included me in their family vacations, and have always lovingly welcomed me into the lives of their kids, Bob and Jeannine, as well as their grandkids. To this day I often claim them as my own.

My nephew Bob, just ten years younger than I, was like my little brother. Bob was game to do whatever cockamamie thing I thought up. Football on the front lawn ended only when he was 16 and playing on his high school team. He knocked me flat on my back where I remained until air returned to my lungs. Like his parents, he has shared his kids without reservation. Bob and Jenny's girls, Heather and Erin, continue to make trips to San Clemente, much to our delight. Heather is a graduate of U.C.S.B. (Santa Barbara) and Erin is beginning her sophomore year at the same esteemed institution, much to Aunt Gerri's delight, as UCSB is her Alma Mater, and their father's, as well.

My niece Jeannine and husband Harry also allowed their kids to spend extended periods of time with Aunt Marg and Aunt Gerri. Jeannine and Harry (hard working teacher and sheep breeder extraordinaire) have followed the family tradition of being great parents and raising great kids. Great-niece Jessica graduated from UC Davis this year and is beginning graduate studies at Texas A & M. Great-nephew Brian is a senior in high school and takes after his two grandfathers as a Fisherman Extraordinaire. My entire family loves to fish. You might say that for my family, baiting a hook is a rite of passage.

My brother John, who tolerated his little sister, allowed me to ride in his car if I lay on the floor in the back so that none of his friends would see me. In later years he allowed me to be part of his pit crew when he was racing Formula Vees, which made me feel very important and proud.

John and my sister-in-law Julie have also shared their kids and grandkids with Aunt Marg. My nephew Christopher and his brother Shawn shared many memorable trips to San Clemente. There were scarcely enough hours in the day for all of our activities—fishing, kayaking, boogie boarding. Etched in my mind forever is Shawn's offer to be our slave if we would allow him to live in our closet. Christopher and his wife Nicole are now the proud parents of Aidan and Ava. Shawn and Katie are loving parents of Violet. New little lives bring light to each of our lives.

My family has always been and continues to be the Salt and Light in my life, yet they are not alone. In each of our lives, there are individuals and even groups of people who inspire us to be all that we can be—people who keep us inspired and growing, and who motivate us to care about others and reflect the Light of God that is within us.

My heart is full of gratitude and love for my family, including Gerri's brother Jim, whom I also claim as my own, along with his family.

Colleagues and students at Watsonville High School; Seminary professors and classmates; the people of First Lutheran Church in Oakland, California where I grew up; Immanuel Lutheran Church in Portland, Oregon, where I did my internship; Lutheran Church of the Cross in Arcadia, California, where I began my work as an ordained pastor; Christ Lutheran Church in San Clemente, California, where I served for nearly twenty years; Spirit of Peace Lutheran Church in Big Bear Lake, California, where I am a member today; and Community Lutheran Church in Rancho Santa Margarita, California, where I served for three months following my retirement—all of you have been Salt and Light in my life.

Throughout the years a host of encouraging and loving friends have supported my journey of faith, shared adventures, and always brought joy and light into my life. Lastly, those who sat on the rocks at Beach Church gave me courage and joined all those who, for me, have been Salt and Light for my journey into the Heart of God.

Thank you, thank you, thank you!!

Pastor Margaret
Marg
Margie